D0638523

who knew?™

HOUSEHOLD SHORTCUTS

who knew?™

HOUSEHOLD SHORTCUTS

Thousands of Clever Fixes for Life's Little Hassles

BRUCE LUBIN & JEANNE BOSSOLINA-LUBIN

Dedication

To Jack, Terrence, and Aidan, as always.

Acknowledgments

Thanks to Jennifer Boudinot, Heather Rodino, Lindsay Herman, and everyone on team Who Knew?! Extra special thanks to Melissa Grover and Todd Vanek at Bang Printing.

Cover design by Lynne Yeamans
Layout and interior design by Susan Livingston

Castle Point Publishing
58 Ninth Street
Hoboken, NJ 07030
www.castlepointpub.com

ISBN: 978-0-9883264-7-7

Printed and bound in the United States of America

2 4 6 8 10 9 7 5 3 1

Please visit us online at www.WhoKnewTips.com

Contents

Introduction

We'll admit it, we love being know-it-alls. Not the kind of know-it-alls who brag, of course, but the kind who always seem to know just how to solve a problem the second it springs up.

While it's true that Bruce will never get sick of showing off his latest DIY concoction to repel bugs at our barbecues, what we really love is knowing how to do things like stop our son's motion sickness with a lemon (page 354), make an emergency black-out candle with a stick of butter (page 43), or even just bring a shrunken sweater back to life (page 26). We've spent years gathering and testing thousands of such tips, and we hope you find them as useful as we do. In this all-new compilation, you'll also find some ideas that inspire you to "DIY," finally tackle that home repair project or pest problem, and maybe even have a homemade spa day when you're done. (And if you don't get that far, at least you'll find out how to get that stain out of your rug!)

After the amazing success of our last book, *Who Knew? 10,001 Easy Solutions to Everyday Problems*, we heard from readers across the US who had questions about all kinds of household problems. So in each chapter, we've included sidebars of the biggest questions about that topic. Don't forget to visit us at WhoKnewTips.com or Facebook.com/WhoknewTips to ask us your questions, too!

Thriftily Yours,
Bruce and Jeanne

chapter 1

Everyday Problems, Solved!

Simple Solutions for Everyday Hassles

Easy Answers for Accidents and Broken Items

Run Out? No Problem

Preventable Problems

In Case of Emergency

Simple Solutions for Everyday Hassles

Memory Maintainer Trying to remember a phone number or other piece of information? Try writing it out by hand several times. Your brain will associate the information with the motor memory of writing it, which will help activate what's known as "working memory," making it easier to remember.

Use Your Fingers to Make Reading Glasses If you're out and realize you forgot your reading glasses, you can use your fingers to create a pinhole lens, which will increase magnification and bring fine print into focus. Don't believe us? Try it! Using one hand, lightly pinch together your thumb and index finger. Allow your middle finger to rest on your thumb under the index finger, creating a small opening between the index and middle fingers. Now hold this opening about an inch from your eye, and adjust it until the object comes in focus. To increase magnification you can use both hands, one in front of each eye. Obviously, you wouldn't want to read an entire contract like this, but it might come in handy for a restaurant menu!

Stopgap Storage for Glasses If you've lost the case for your glasses, create a makeshift one with an empty paper towel roll. Cut it to the length of your glasses, and cover one end with duct tape. It will keep your glasses scratch-free until you can get a new case.

Who Knew? Classic Tip

Lost a contact lens and can't seem to find it anywhere? Turn off the lights and turn on a flashlight. Sweep it over the area where you lost it and the lens will reflect the light.

Fix Stuck Plugs If an electric plug on an appliance fits too snugly and is difficult to pull out, rub its prongs with a soft lead pencil, and it will move in and out more easily.

Fix a Kinky Cord If you have teenagers who always seem to have headphones on, they'll love this trick. If your headphone cords are hopelessly kinked and tangled, wrap them gently around the outside of a coffee mug several times, then tape them so they're held close to the sides. Next, fill the mug with boiling water and let sit. By the time the water has cooled, the warmth will have unkinked the cords.

Earbud Answer Thanks to the iPod, earbud headphones are more popular than ever. But for some of us, it seems like they're always falling out of our ears! Help them stay in with this simple trick: Run the cord behind your neck before putting the buds in your ears. This will make it hard for them to become dislodged.

Pump Up the Volume Have trouble hearing music through your mobile device's speakers? Just place it in a bowl (preferably an aluminum or stainless steel one). The sides of the bowl with amplify the sound.

Pesky Packaging How-to Don't risk cutting your hands on that thick plastic packaging used for gadgets and electronics. Most household scissors won't do the job well, but luckily, we've found an even better tool—a handheld can opener! Simply run the plastic through the can opener as you would a tin can, and it'll slice right open, hassle-free!

Unstick a Stubborn Lightbulb Got a lightbulb stuck in its socket? Avoid breaking both the bulb and the socket by making two "handles" out of duct tape that you can use to twist the broken bulb out—this also works great if you've accidentally shattered the bulb in the socket. First, cut a foot-long length of duct tape and stick the ends of the

who knew? THE BIG QUESTION

Removing Stickers and Labels

How do I get a sticky label off of something?

—Kathryn Gatineau, via Facebook

Mayo Method Removing a stubborn sticker or label can be so frustrating! Believe it or not, mayonnaise can help. To remove the gummy remains of a label or sticker on a window or a mirror (or anything else that won't stain), cover it with mayonnaise and let it sit for five to 10 minutes, then gently scrape off with a putty knife.

Witch Hazel Help Witch hazel is an inexpensive astringent found at most drugstores. Use it to get rid of labels by soaking a cotton ball in it. Hold it on the spot for a few minutes, and then rub the goo away.

Hand Santizer How-to The alcohol in hand sanitizer works to unstick the adhesive in the sticker glue. Just rub a bit into the spot and let it sit for a couple minutes, then use a coin to scrape it off.

Call in the Big Guns Still can't get that label off? Try using a hair dryer! Run it over the label for several minutes, then peel right off. The heat warms the adhesive, making it less sticky.

strip together to form a big loop, adhesive side in. Place the loop around the bulb, so that the bulb is at its center. Then bring the two sides of the loop together, allowing the tape to stick to itself and form two long ends of tape on either side: these are your "handles." Grab them between your thumbs and forefingers, and gently twist counter-clockwise to unscrew the bulb.

Nifty Knot Remover We've untangled the knottiest of knots with this surprising helper—cornstarch. Work small amounts of cornstarch into knotted chain jewelry, shoe-laces, and string. Seriously, who knew?

Who Knew? Classic Tip

To light hard-to-reach wicks at the bottom of jar candles, use an uncooked strand of spaghetti. Light the end of it, then use it like a fireplace match.

Key Ring Assistance A staple remover is one of those gizmos you own, but rarely use, so it's nice it has a second use around the house: helping put new keys on a key ring. Pinch the staple remover so that its claws divide the rings for you, and you won't have to sacrifice a fingernail!

Good to the Last Drop Your days of being driven crazy trying to get that last little bit of liquid out of a spray bottle are over! If you remove the plastic straw, tightly close the lid, and squeeze the handle with the bottle turned upside down, you'll never waste a drop again!

The Last Bit of Samples If you've taken advantage of various freebie offers online, you probably have a lot of free samples of lotion, moisturizer, and other beauty products. To make sure you're getting every last bit, just snip off the top of the plastic tube before you're done. Then you can reach a finger inside and scoop up the last of your free cosmetics!

Give Pants a Little More "Give" Pants feeling a little too "fitted" lately? (Don't worry, we won't come right out and say you've gained weight.) To add about ½ inch more room in the waist, try this rubber band quick fix: When your pants are on, slip a rubber band over the button, poke the other end through the buttonhole, and loop it around and over the button again to close. An elastic hair band will do the trick, too.

Erase Deodorant Streaks Have you ever gotten deodorant on your shirt while dressing in the morning? Next time you have pantyhose with a run, save them for this easy fix. Just rub the pantyhose onto the white mark and it will disappear!

Journey of 1,000 Untied Shoes Do your shoelaces keep getting untied? Just rub some ChapStick onto the laces and they'll stay put.

Who Knew? Classic Tip

Having the drawstring completely come out of a hoodie or yoga pants doesn't have to be a clothing calamity anymore! Just grab a straw, thread the string through it, then staple one end so they'll stay together. Use the straw as a giant needle to guide the drawstring back where it belongs.

Eradicate Static in a Snap Here's a quick fix for clothes plagued by annoying static cling: Squirt a couple drops of lotion onto your hands, then smooth it over the garments.

See Also . . . For all-natural ways to get rid of common stains, check out the Stain Solutions and Laundry Tips chapter.

Open Jars with Ease Struggling to open a jar? Grab a screwdriver! Place the tip of a flat-head screwdriver under the edge of the lid, and turn the jar gently until you hear a little pop. This means that the vacuum seal has been broken, and you'll be able to open the jar easily.

Good-bye, Gummy Hair Your child came home from school with gum in her hair—now what? Before you get out the scissors, try this technique. Make a paste by slowing adding water to baking soda, then add a bit more water so the consistency is more of a slurry. Then rub the mixture into the hair and begin to work out the gum, adding more slurry if necessary. Once the graininess of the baking soda has helped you get out the sticky gum, wash the baking soda mess out of the hair with your regular shampoo.

All the Newly Single Ladies A stuck ring can be gently wriggled off by coating the finger with lip balm around the ring itself. As for why you frantically need the ring off your finger—who are we to judge?

Get Rid of Garlic Breath That garlic bread you had at dinner was delicious, but now no one will get close to you! To neutralize breath odor after a garlicky meal, mix together a tablespoon or two of lemon juice with a pinch of sugar. Swirl it around your mouth and then swallow it. It will neutralize the smell so you can breathe out without fear!

Plastic Wrap Pointer When you're stuck in the kitchen trying to find the end of your plastic wrap, try this quick tape trick: Stick a small piece of tape to the plastic and pull away from the roll. The end should lift up easily.

Cling Wrap Won't Cling? Plastic wrap sure is handy, except when it refuses to stick! If you're having trouble getting it to adhere to a bowl or casserole dish, first put a little water on the sides. The water will form a seal that will help it cling.

For a Perfectly Sharp Paring Knife To quickly sharpen a paring knife without special tools, run the edge along the strike panel of a matchbox. Repeat on both sides until you reach the desired sharpness.

Makeshift Cork Here's a great use for those short candlestick ends you haven't thrown out . . . because you were waiting for someone to tell you a great use for them. If you have an unfinished bottle of wine but you've lost or broken the cork, heat a one-inch candle end in a glass container in the microwave for three seconds on high. It will soften it up enough to stick in the bottle and serve as a stopper.

See Also . . . For ways to solve common cooking mishaps, check out the Clever Cooking Tips chapter.

Who Knew? Classic Tip

If you've been fussing with a drawer that won't open, it's probably expanded due to humidity. Dry it out with a hair dryer set on low heat, or place a work lamp with a 60-watt bulb nearby and leave for 30 minutes. The drawer will contract, and you'll be able to move it easily again.

An Open and Shut Case Ever find yourself tugging at a stuck kitchen or medicine cabinet? It may be that the magnet that holds the door shut is too strong. The fix is simple: Stick a piece of tape on the magnet. The tape will weaken the magnetic pull, making the door easier to open.

Steady Does It Friends are coming over for dinner, and you just noticed a wobble in the dining room table. Fix it in a jiffy with a piece of cork. Cut a piece to the right height to stop the wobble and then attach it to the bottom of the leg with wood glue. The table will be steady and as a bonus, the cork will protect your floor!

Stop Sliding Around Stop your mattress from sliding around by placing a rug pad on top of the box spring. Available in most big-box discount stores, these anti-skid pads can be cut to fit, so that they'll provide invisible traction, keeping your mattress where it belongs.

Who Knew? Classic Tip

Don't spend money on a no-slip mat for underneath your rug. Grab a caulking gun (or a friend who has one) and apply acrylic-latex caulk to the underside. Run the caulk in lines that run the width of the rug and are about six inches apart and it will never slip again!

Felt Fix Have a cabinet that makes you cringe every time it bangs shut? Glue a little piece of felt to the inside of the door so that it closes more quietly from now on.

Flat Cushion Fix The beautiful cushions on your chairs are so flat they're not much more than decoration at this point—now what? Let them sit in the sun for several

who knew? THE BIG QUESTION

Hanging Picture Frames

I'm redoing my hallway and have a ton of picture to hang. Any tips to make it easier? I feel like every time I hang pictures it turns into a disaster! **—JoAnn Smith Montes, via Facebook**

Have a Plan It's hard to tell what your pictures are going to look like on the wall before you hang them. Solve this problem with the help of some cardboard. Using your picture frame as a stencil, outline the frame onto the cardboard, then cut it. Once you have stand-ins for each item you're hanging, tape them up on the wall to simulate what your frames will look like in the space. Once everything's perfect, mark the spot on the wall with a pencil.

Hang Pictures Easily To get rid of the guesswork that comes with putting a nail in the wall, try this trick. Place a dab of toothpaste on the back of the frame on the hook or string (whatever will touch the nail). Hold the frame up to the wall, position it carefully, and press it to the wall. The toothpaste will leave a mark that you can hammer a nail through.

Picture Perfect If you only have a few frames to hang, you'll love this trick to make sure you drill the holes exactly where you want them. Photocopy the back of the item you want to hang, and tape it on the wall. Then drill into the paper wherever the hook or hole is on the photocopy! This is an especially good tip when mounting things that need multiple screws in specific places, like wall-mounted electronics.

hours (flipping halfway through) and they'll fluff back up! The sun's warmth is just enough heat to evaporate cushion-flattening moisture, but not enough to damage them (just don't leave them out so long they fade!).

Easy Answers for Accidents and Broken Items

Rescue a Stuck DVD If your DVD player is holding a DVD hostage and won't spit it out, you may be able to fix it yourself without heading to the repair shop. Look next to the tray that holds the DVD for a tiny hole, then stick the end of an unfolded paperclip into it. It should activate the player's emergency tray opener, allowing you to stick another DVD in there and try again.

Skipping CD Saver If you have a CD or DVD that's started to skip, it's ChapStick to the rescue! Wash the disc with soapy water and dry with a paper towel or soft cloth. Then rub the lip balm on the scratch, and wipe off the excess with a dry paper towel or cloth. It will now jump over that part of the disc cleanly, without causing an annoying skip that has you running over to your CD player.

Bring Your Phone Back to Life Left your cell phone in your hot car, and now it won't work? Just turn on the car's air conditioner, and direct it at the phone. When you get home, continue cooling the phone until it is no longer hot to the touch, and then put it in an airtight bag and stow it in the fridge (not freezer) for five minutes. Your phone should work fine again now!

Who Knew? Classic Tip

Here's a trick that could save you hundreds: If your cell phone gets wet, first take the battery out and dry it with a paper towel. Then bury the phone and the battery in a bowl of uncooked rice for 24 hours. The rice will draw the rest of the water out of the phone, and hopefully it will be back in business again.

Retractable Cord Keeper If the retractable cord on your vacuum cleaner or other electronic device won't lock properly, try placing a clothespin on the cord near the opening on the machine. It will clip the cord at your desired length and prevent any preemptive retracting.

Broken Toy? If you have an electronic toy whose batteries are loose due to a missing spring, don't throw it away or pay to get it fixed. Simply ball up a small amount of aluminum foil and put it in the spring's place. The aluminum will conduct electricity in lieu of the spring.

Who Knew? Classic Tip

If you shatter something made out of glass on your floor, try out this crafty tip. Dampen a piece of white bread, and dab it on the glass fragments. It's much more effective than using a broom.

Find Leaking Air Easily If your inflatable mattress or other blow-up item has a leak, but you're not sure where it is, use this trick to find the hole. Make some soapy water by adding dishwashing liquid to water, then pour it over the inflated mattress. Even if the hole is tiny, you should see small bubbles forming around it as you push on the mattress. Flip the mattress over and repeat to find any holes on the opposite side.

Get the Dents Out of a Ping-Pong Ball The sound of ping-pong balls being paddled all over the basement is worth every minute if it's keeping your kids busy! Unfortunately, when the kids finally emerge from downstairs, you notice that the balls are filled with dents. To get the balls round again, fill a jar to the brim with warm water, then place the balls inside and close the lid so that they're submerged. In 20 minutes or less, the water's warmth will make them pop back into place.

Revive Wet Pages We hate it when we accidentally get books wet—the pages stick together and will easily tear. But it doesn't have to mean the book is ruined! You can save it by carefully inserting paper towels between the soggy pages. As the paper towels get damp, replace them with dry ones, until the book has completely dried out.

Who Knew? Classic Tip

If your sunglasses have gotten completely twisted, don't throw them out. Just turn a hair dryer on high and aim it at your frames. The heat makes the plastic arms flexible enough for you to gently bend them back to their original shape.

Seamless Sunglasses Light scratches in the plastic lenses of your sunglasses can be easily fixed. Just spray a bit of wood furniture polish, like Pledge, onto the scratch, then wipe away the extra with a paper towel or soft cloth. The polish will fill the scratch and make your sunglasses like new!

Stuck Photos? If your photographs are stuck to each other or to a glass frame, the solution is steam. Use a steamer, a steam iron set on its highest setting, or a pan of boiling water to get steam as close as you can between the photo and whatever it's stuck to (being careful not to burn yourself). As the photo gets warmer and wetter, it should become easy to peel away. Lay out to dry, then flatten with a fat book if it has curled.

Who Knew? Classic Tip

If you've accidentally shrunk a sweater in the dryer, there may still be hope. Let it sit in a bucket of water with a generous amount of hair conditioner mixed in. The chemicals in the conditioner can untangle the fibers in your sweater, making them expand back to their original condition. If that doesn't work, it's time to cut up the sweater and make some new mittens!

Revive Water-Resistant Items Do you have a jacket, backpack, or tent that used to be water resistant but has lost its effectiveness over time? Set your hair dryer to its highest setting and blow air evenly over it. The warmth will reactivate the coating on the cloth that makes it repel water.

Zipper Zip-Up If the zipper breaks on your pants, try this fantastic quick fix: Wind the loop of a key ring through the notch in your zipper, then loop it over the button to close.

Cuff 'Em Are the cuffs of your favorite sweater starting to get stretched out? Make them like new again by blowing them with hot air from your hair dryer! Just wet the cuffs with water, set the hair dryer on its highest setting, and then blow-dry until no longer wet. The heat will shrink the cuffs slightly, bringing them back down to the right size.

Twine Time If you have a pair of espadrilles whose heels are looking ragged, patch them up with everyday brown twine you can find at the hardware store. Cut the twine into pieces that fit in the gaps and adhere with shoe glue.

Remove Water from Your Watch If you've ever seen condensation under your watch face, you know how frustrating it can be! Luckily, there's a solution. Simply strap the watch to a lightbulb and turn it on for a few minutes. The heat from the bulb is the perfect amount to make the water disappear.

Rescue Dropped Jewelry If you accidentally drop a piece of jewelry down your sink's drain, don't panic.

Immediately turn off the water (if it's on) and go get your vacuum. Place a piece of pantyhose over the end of the hose and secure it with a rubber band. Then hold the vacuum over the drain and turn it on. If you're lucky, the suction will pull up your piece of jewelry and catch it in the nylon. It's worth a shot before you call a plumber!

Who Knew? Classic Tip

If a stone has popped out of a piece of your jewelry and you were lucky enough to save it, you can easily put it back in place with a tiny dab of clear nail polish.

Powder Preserver Oh no! You just dropped your compact, and now your powder is in a million tiny pieces. To get any kind of powder makeup (such as foundation, eye shadow, or blush) back together again, add a few drops of rubbing alcohol to the fine dust, then push it back together with the back of a spoon. Your powder will become pressed again!

Fluff with a Fork To remove dents in your carpet left by furniture, fluff the fibers back into shape using a fork. Simply stick the tines into the fibers and brush them straight up.

Got Gum on Your Sofa? Here's another great reason to keep duct tape around the house: It can get rid of gum! To remove gum from upholstery, wrap a piece of duct tape around your fingers, with the sticky side facing out. Then, with a quick motion, press onto the gum and lift. Repeat until all of the gum is gone.

Fix Up Wood Furniture Does your wooden coffee table, dresser, or dining room furniture have visible scratches? No sweat! Use a similarly hued shoe polish to fill in the offending marks, and voilà—like new!

Wooden Dent Removal As long as the wood hasn't broken apart underneath, you may be able to fix dents in wooden floors or furniture. Here's how: Run a rag under warm water and wring it out, then place it on top of the dent. Apply an iron set on medium heat to the rag until the rag dries out. Repeat this process until your dent is gone.

Toothpaste for Tile Touch-Ups Scuffs and scratches on the linoleum tiles got you down? A simple solution is at your fingertips: Reach into the bathroom cabinet for some white toothpaste, and apply to the scuffs using a soft cloth. Wipe away with a clean, dampened cloth.

Fix Your Flooring If your vinyl flooring is coming up, put it back where it belongs! Lay a sheet of foil on top (shiny side down), then run a hot iron over it several times until you feel the glue on the bottom of the tile starting to melt again. Place something heavy, like a stack of books, on top and leave it overnight to set.

See Also . . . For tricks for making home repairs easier, check out the Home-Repair Hints chapter.

Good-bye, Broken Blinds Vertical blinds can be pricey, so it's incredibly frustrating when one of the holes in the plastic slats gets ripped open, causing all or part of the slat to fall off. It turns out the fix to this common blinds problem is quite simple: Use a paperclip! Use a paperclip to bridge the gap over the ripped part of the slat, then superglue the slat back together while paperclip is holding it in place.

Get Marker Off Your Wall While you weren't looking, your child stopped drawing on the construction paper you gave him and decided to take his markers to a bigger canvas: your walls! Thankfully, you can remove the marks with rubbing alcohol. Just dampen a cloth and rub until the marker is gone.

Easy Glue Removal If your gluing project gets a little messy, use WD-40 to lift off dried glue spots from any hard surfaces you work on. Wipe clean, and get back to arts and crafts.

Who Knew? Classic Tip

Superglue's claim to fame is that it sticks to everything—and is impossible to get off. But if you accidentally get some on your work project or even your fingers, there is one substance that can get you out of your "bind." Soak the corner of a soft cloth or paper towel in nail polish remover, then hold it on the area until the glue dissolves. Be aware, however, that nail polish remover will eat away at varnish and other finishes.

Wipe Away Crayon Marks with Toothpaste Your little artist has created a beautiful work of art for you—on the living room wall! To remove his "art," put some toothpaste on a dry sponge, and rub the mess in a circular motion. Allow the toothpaste to sit for five minutes, then use a damp washcloth to wipe away the paste. The white, non-gel variety of toothpaste works best. (Of course, test first on an inconspicuous area to make sure it won't hurt your paint job.)

Glue Gadget Wood veneer on a piece of furniture peeling? Glue down the fragile surface without having to lift up any more of the veneer by using a drinking straw. Flatten the straw, then dip the end in wood glue and slip it under the part that's peeling. Then gently blow into the other end to dispense a tiny amount of glue.

Run Out? No Problem

More Battery Juice You've just realized your cell phone's battery is about to die, but you're at work and don't have your charger. Get a little more talk time by detaching the battery and placing it in your workplace's freezer, then allowing it to come back up to room temperature before you use it. The cold will keep your battery from losing a single drop of juice before you use it.

Revive a Dead Pen There's no need to throw away a pen that's stopped writing long before it should have. Just get rid of the dried-up ink clogging its point by boiling water, then removing the water from the heat and dipping the pen tip into it for 10 seconds.

Make Ink Last You're trying to print out a document, but you just ran out of ink! This solution will save you a trip to the store: Take out the ink cartridge, then blow hot air on it with a hair dryer. Once it's warm, put it back in the printer. The heat loosens the ink that is stuck to the side of the cartridge, often giving you enough to finish the job.

Out of Dish Soap? You just noticed that you're out of dishwasher detergent, but you don't want to get in the car and run to the supermarket. You know you can't use regular dishwashing liquid because of the suds, so what can you use? The secret: shampoo. Shampoo will cut through tough grease just like your normal detergent, and won't get too sudsy for your machine. Just be sure to stick to shampoo only, not one of those two-in-one shampoo and conditioners. And don't tell your family what you've done if you don't want to get any weird looks!

Surprising Deodorant Substitutes If you've run out of deodorant, don't worry! You can still leave the house without fear of a stinky sweat smell: Apple cider vinegar or antiseptic mouthwash both make great substitutions for deodorant in a pinch. Saturate a cloth with the vinegar or mouthwash, and rub it under your arms.

Hair Gel-O? Run out of hair gel? Head to the kitchen cabinet and grab some unflavored gelatin. Mix 2 teaspoons gelatin with 1 cup warm water, and stick the mixture in the refrigerator. Once it's set, you can use it as you would regular hair gel. Who knew?

Cornstarch Helper If you run out of shampoo, use a homemade "dry" shampoo instead: cornstarch. Shake a little where your hair is parted, let it sit for a minute or two, then flip your head upside-down and massage it out.

Preventable Problems

Keep Cords and Wires in Shape Thanks to gravity and lots of use, electrical cords tend to fray and break off around their plug ends. (Anyone with a Mac-brand laptop has experience with frayed charger wires.) Not only is this irritating, but the exposed wiring can be dangerous. To prevent damaged and frayed cords, we've found this nifty trick to be very effective: Dismantle a pen and grab the tiny metal spring inside. Wrap the spring around the end of your cord—this will hold it straight and keep the wire's covering from bending and breaking.

Proactive Electronics Protection You probably know that leaving electronics in a hot car can hurt them, but did you know that extreme cold can harm them too? The freezing temperatures cause their tiny components to become brittle, making them much easier to break. If you live in a cold area, make sure to bring your electronics inside during winter!

A Hot Tip for Take-Out Do you have a seat warmer in your car? Whenever you pick up a pizza for dinner, turn on the warmer to help the food stay toasty on the way home. And make sure to tell your family so they can admire your genius!

Don't Track Food on Your Track Pad If you make a habit of eating while working on your laptop, protect your track pad from sticky and greasy fingers. Cover it temporarily with a Post-it note! You'll still be able to use the track pad through the piece of paper, and it will stay much cleaner.

The Great Tape Tip Can't find the end to a roll of tape? It's annoying, we know! Here's how you can prepare for next time: Simply reuse the plastic tag that comes with a bagged loaf of bread. Stick it to the tape's end, and voila! Next time you need some tape, you'll have no problem.

Smooth-Moving Lids To stop the lids of honey, molasses, and other sweet stuff from sticking, rub a little petroleum jelly on the rim of the jar when you first open it. The petroleum jelly will lubricate the threads of the jar so it won't stick anymore.

Who Knew? Classic Tip

Nothing gets the summertime party going faster than firing up the backyard grill. Just make sure you keep all that smoked and grilled meat coming—it's unforgivable to run out of fuel before the last kebab is bobbed. Even without a gas gauge, there is a way to figure out how much fuel you have left. Here's what to do a day or two *before* the flip-flopped masses are set to arrive. Boil water, then pour it down the side of the tank. Place your hand on the side: the cool part has propane inside, and the warm part is empty.

Oh, the Humidity! To give your houseplants a little extra humidity, especially in dry climates or in winter, place their pots on a tray of pebbles and add some water. The water will slowly evaporate, adding moisture to the plants. And the tray of pebbles will look decorative too!

Draft Dodger You probably know that your houseplant doesn't appreciate being left in cold areas, but did you know that fluctuating temperatures can harm them too? In the winter, keep your plants out of drafty areas, such as near the front door. They'll grow better in warmer areas that don't change temperatures as often.

Not Blowing in the Wind You don't have to tie up flyaway curtains to get them to stay in place. A marble or a few coins sewn into the lining will keep them weighted down for a more elegant look. In some cases you can simply drop the coins or marbles inside. If the hem is sewn shut you can make a little split, drop the weights in, and sew the lining back up.

Stop Coaster Condensation You've laid out coasters to keep your table safe, but in the hot summer months they keep sticking to the bottom of your glass, thanks to all the condensation! Solve the problem with a little bit of salt. Just sprinkle it on the coaster and your glass won't stick!

Protect Family Photos Problem: you want to hang family pictures on a corkboard at home or at work, but you don't want to damage the photos with a pushpin. Solution? Use paperclips! Tack a number of paperclips to the board using pushpins, then slide your pictures into the paperclips. They'll stay in place, and you won't have a put holes in the photos.

Polish Snags to Save Hangers Notice some nicks in your wooden or plastic hangers? Prevent snags in your clothes (and save the hangers) by brushing them with a light coat of nail polish.

Prevent Pantyhose Runs Weird but true: Freezing panty hose can keep them from running. Before wearing a pair of nylons for the first time, stick them in the freezer overnight. The cold strengthens the fibers, which will keep them from running.

New Shoes without the Blisters Breaking in new shoes doesn't have to mean painful blisters. Rub a bit of gel antiperspirant on your feet in the places where you normally get blisters, and get ready to enjoy your night out! The antiperspirant will keep friction-causing moisture away, while creating a seal around your skin that keeps blisters at bay.

Up Against the Wall Protect your walls from the dings and scratches picture frames can leave behind. Whenever

THE BIG QUESTION who knew?

Making Mending Easier

Do you have any great sewing tips?
—Emily Porter, via Whoknewtips.com

Use a Dryer Sheet One of the most common (and irritating) sewing mishaps is tangled thread. So, before you begin a sewing project, stick a threaded needle through a dryer sheet, which will help prevent knotty messes.

No-Stress Needle-Threading For easier threading, stiffen the ends of your thread by applying a light spritz of hair spray. The strengthened thread won't fray and will easily slip through the eye of your needle.

Thick Fabric Trick If a pin or needle will not easily penetrate thick fabric, this little household trick will make sewing a cinch: Simply stick the pin into a bar of soap to make it nice and slippery.

Make Sleeves and Pant Legs Easy If you're mending a hole on a sleeve or pant leg, it's easy to miss a stitch when the fabric gets all balled up. Make your job easier by rolling up a magazine and placing it inside. It will partially unroll as far as the sleeve or leg will let it, creating just enough tension to hold the fabric in place.

Sharpen a Dull Needle If your needle has grown dull, sharpen it up again by running its tip back and forth on an emery board several times!

you hang a framed picture or photo, grab two packing peanuts and slice them in half lengthwise. Then glue them to the corners on the back side of the frame. The Styrofoam will protect your walls from scratches every time you adjust the frame (or bump into it on your way down the hallway).

Add Grip to Your Slippers Are your cozy slippers too slippery on tile or hardwood floors? Don't slide around the house and risk wipeouts—just add grippers to the bottoms yourself! All you need is a hot-glue gun: Apply glue in straight lines or dots or any pattern you like, let it dry, and your slippers will be nonslip!

See Also . . . For clothing storage solutions, see the Keeping Away Clutter chapter.

Perfume Storage Secret Perfume is very volatile—the fragrance breaks down rapidly when exposed to heat and air. If you're not going to use the entire bottle within 30 days, store it in the refrigerator to extend its life.

Rubber Band Bottle Identifier Use rubber bands to find the right shampoo, conditioner, and body wash bottles while you're soapy-eyed in the shower. Just slide a rubber band on the base of the bottle, and feel for it! If your bottles are similar in shape, place the rubber bands at different places on the bottles.

In Case of Emergency

Never Get Locked Out Again Looking for a place to store a spare key? Try your wallet. Place a spare key between two old gift cards, and tape the edges shut. You'll be able to store the key easily in your wallet, since it will fit perfectly in one of the credit card slots.

Ingenious Hiding Hole Keeping a spare key to your home under your doormat sure is convenient, but it's also a bit obvious. Instead, bury the key underground in a container with a rock attached to the lid. But don't spend $10 or more for one in a catalog. Instead, make your own by using superglue to attach a rock to the lid of an old pill bottle. Bury the bottle under a backyard bush or somewhere else inconspicuous.

How to Hide a PIN Where's a safe place to keep PINs for bank and credit cards? The answer isn't so much where as how: Hide them inside a fake phone number. For example, if your PIN is 1234 (and hopefully, it isn't!), scribble 347-1234 on the inside of your day planner or somewhere else accessible. Would-be thieves won't know it's the number they're looking for.

Who Knew? Classic Tip

Here's an ingenious idea for keeping valuables safe from burglars: Wash out an old mayonnaise jar and paint the inside of it white. Let the paint dry and then place your money, jewelry, and other items inside. Store it in the back of your fridge, and it'll still be there even if you're burglarized.

Stash Cash the MacGyver Way We love this super-clever idea for safely storing emergency cash—in an old ChapStick container! To reuse a tube, first twist the bottom ring so the lip balm rises all the way out through the top. Remove the balm and its plastic container. Then, remove the bottom cap and clean everything out. The bottom cap will have a thin stick attached to it, which held the balm inside the tube. Cut off this stick so you can fit your cash inside. Replace the bottom cap on the tube, insert your rolled-up cash through the top, and pop on the lid. Eat your heart out, MacGyver!

Beat a Blackout with a Butter Candle We love this Boy Scout–worthy tip for lighting emergencies. If you lose power and don't have any candles, reach into the fridge for a stick of butter and grab a short strip of toilet paper. Cut off ¼ of a full stick of butter (2 tablespoons), leaving the wrapper on. Cut or tear one square of toilet paper into quarters; fold one-quarter square along the diagonal, and roll it into a wick. Fold the wick at the bottom to suit the height of the butter "candle:" You want about ¼ inch of wick extending above the top of the candle. Holding the butter upright, poke a hole through the center with a toothpick or skewer to fit the wick. Use the skewer to insert the wick through the hole, leaving that ¼ inch at the top. Rub a bit of butter onto the starter wick until it's coated, and then your butter candle is ready to light! Each 2-ounce candle will burn for about four hours. If you like, place your candle in a glass to keep your tabletop clean and avoid any dangerous mishaps.

Emergency Candles in an Instant If you're ever in need of a last-minute light source, think Crisco! The tub of shortening makes a great, long-lasting emergency candle. Just cut a piece of string (or wick) so it's slightly taller than the tub, stick it in the center, and light it—your makeshift candle will last around 45 days!

chapter 2

Home-Repair Hints

Tips for Tools

Easy Prep, Easy Cleanup

Doors and Windows

Walls

Painting Pointers

Wallpaper and Shelf Liners

Plumbing and Pipes

Outdoor Projects

Tips for Tools

Tip-Top Tools Next time you get a new pair of shoes or another product with a packet of silica gel inside, save the packet and stash it in your toolbox. Silica gel is a desiccant, which absorbs moisture and draws it away from your tools, preventing oxidation (i.e., rusting). You can also use a piece of chalk.

Who Knew? Classic Tip

When you buy a rust remover, what you're really paying for is phosphoric acid. However, phosphoric acid can also be found in something you probably have around the house—cola. Dip tools, screws, or anything else that needs de-rusting into cola and leave for several minutes. Then scrub away the black substance that remains and repeat if necessary.

A Safer Toolbox If you've ever jabbed or scratched your hand while digging around your toolbox, you'll love this tip. (Plus it's a great way of reusing those Styrofoam packing peanuts that you always seem to be throwing out.) Poke any tool that has a sharp or pointy edge into one of the peanuts before storing. The next time you're hunting for that Phillips head screwdriver, you won't get an unpleasant stab from the needle-nose pliers!

The Rubber Band Trick Removing a nail? Wrap a rubber band or two around the claw end of the hammer. The band will protect the wall from scratches or nicks while you pull out the nail.

Hair Comb Hammer Trick If you're hammering in a nail, protect your fingers from a pounding with this crafty tip. Keep nails in place while you hammer by using a thick (and cheap) plastic comb—yep, a comb you'd use on your hair! Just place the comb on your target spot, and slip a nail through two of its tines to hold it steady.

No-Slip Screwdriver Doing housework with a screwdriver? To make the handle less slippery and safer to use, swipe it with chalk before you begin.

Penny Wise A penny won't get you much these days, not even when it comes to penny candy, but it may help to turn a screw. When you don't have a screwdriver on hand, try using a penny if the slot is wide enough.

Crafty Use for Old Gift Cards In need of a thin yet sturdy household tool for scraping grout, repairing holes in walls, or filling scratches in wood? Use a used-up gift card (or expired credit card) for the job—any unusable hard plastic card will do. And if you're anything like us, you have plenty of those!

Sand Your Scissors Sharpen up your scissors in a snap with sandpaper. Just cut a piece of sandpaper at least five times, and the gritty surface will get your scissors' blades back in shape.

Easy Prep, Easy Cleanup

Avoid Wear and Tear During Home Repair Home-repair projects take longer and cause more grief than anyone ever anticipates. Make restoring order to your house a little less of an ordeal by covering vents and ceiling lamps with plastic wrap to protect them during home-repair projects.

Putty Knife If you trash your dirty putty knives after completing every paint or spackle job, you'll appreciate this money- and energy-saver. Before beginning a home-repair project, spritz the putty knife with a light coat of cooking spray. The slippery stuff makes cleanup possible—and even easy. Caked-on paint, spackle, glue, and any other chunks o' gunk will come right off, and your knife will be like new!

Beware the Caulk When caulking the edges of your bathtub, keep in mind that the caulking will often expand and crack the first time you fill the tub with hot water. To combat this, fill the tub with hot water first, then caulk away.

Who Knew? Classic Tip

Most stepladders are perfectly safe, of course, but if you want to amp up the nonskid surface of the rungs, there's an easy way to do it. Just paint the steps of the ladder and, before they dry, sprinkle fine-grained sand on top. The sand will stick to the steps and create a sandpaper-like surface.

Sweep Away Sawdust in a Snap Cleaning up sawdust in your home workshop can be a tricky chore, which is why we love this easy-peasy strategy: Use a dryer sheet! All it takes is one or two swipes on the work surface, and you'll ditch the dust with no hassle.

Doors and Windows

Squeaky Doors Get the Grease Are your doors shrieking every time you open them? Don't run to the store for WD-40. Squeaky doors can be silenced with a little hair conditioner wiped on the offending hinge. Now your entryways will be as tame as your mane.

Who Knew? Classic Tip

If your windows are frosting over, dissolve 1 tablespoon salt in 1 gallon hot water and rub on the panes with a soft cloth. Then wipe away with a dry cloth. This will often keep your windows frost-free.

Temporary Screen Fix Don't leave a hole in your screen door just because you don't have the right tools to fix it. Instead, use rubber cement to affix a small piece of pantyhose around the area. It's easy to remove but will keep ugly flying things out of your house in the meantime (at least the ones that don't live there).

Stop a Door from Sticking Your bedroom door has expanded, and realigning the hinges didn't work. Instead of taking the entire door down to sand the bottom, try this trick instead. Place enough newspaper under the door until it can just barely close on top of it. Then tape a piece of coarse sandpaper on top of the newspaper, and open and close the door until it glides over the floor without a noise.

Grease Up Your Windows Don't pull a muscle trying to shove open a stuck heavy window. Windows will open and close more easily if you occasionally rub a bar of soap across the track.

Walls

Unhelpful Holes? If a hole in your wall (or whatever else you're working on) is too stripped to hold a screw, dab some glue on a tiny piece of steel wool (which can be cut with scissors) and stuff it into the hole. Once the glue dries, you can screw in your screw without a problem.

The Path of Least Resistance Coat a nail or screw with a light layer of lip balm to ease it into the wall before hanging a picture or shelf.

Protect Walls with Tape Planning to hang beautiful family photos or kids' artwork around the house? Before you hammer a nail into your wall, cover the spot with clear tape to prevent the paint from chipping.

Who Knew? Classic Tip

If you're having trouble with your screws falling off your screwdriver as you're trying to get them into the wall, first poke the screw through a piece of plastic wrap. Hold on to the wrap while you're screwing, then pull it away when you're finished.

Got a Screw Loose? You've just struggled to remove a stripped screw from the wall. Now how do you fix the hole? Use a wooden golf tee! First, squirt some wood glue into the hole, then insert the tee as far as it will go, tapping it into place with a hammer. Next, use a utility knife to cut the tee flush with the wall. You've now made a stable base for the new screw. Drill a pilot hole into the golf tee, and insert your new screw. Problem solved!

Finding Imperfections Filling and sanding every hole in the wall before you paint can be enough of a pain, but sometimes it's hard to find every crack, hole, and imperfection. Make your job easier by turning off the lights in

Patching Walls

Is there an easy way to repair holes in the wall made from nails?

—Laura Woolridge, via Facebook

who knew? THE BIG QUESTION

Homemade Spackle Here's an easy, homemade spackle you can make for quick patches: Combine a tablespoon of salt with a tablespoon of cornstarch. Mix them together with just enough water to make a paste. Apply while still wet.

Q-Tip Trick Before spackling small holes in your wall caused by nails, first cut a Q-tip in half and insert in the hole, stick end first. Then spackle as you normally would. The Q-tip will completely fill the hole and ensure you won't have to go back for a second pass.

Soap Up You're moving out of an apartment and need to fill in the holes in the wall caused by nails by the time your landlord shows up to inspect the place. Just grab a bar of white soap and rub across the hole until the soap fills it. It's not a permanent fix, but it will make the walls look clean until they can be repainted.

Quick Patch If you notice tiny marks or paint cracks in a white wall and need a quick fix before your next paint job, run same-color chalk over the offending areas. The chalk should blend right in and hide the cracks in the meantime.

a room, then slowly running a flashlight over the entire surface of the wall. The light will cast different shadows in these areas, making them easier to see than they would have been in the daylight.

Who Knew? Classic Tip

Looking for a stud and don't have a stud finder? Use an electric razor instead. Most razors will change in tone slightly when going over a stud in the wall.

Painting Pointers

Skip the Drip Finally tackling that room that needs to be repainted? Create your own drip-free paintbrush holder with a plastic milk jug. Cut a hole in the side large enough to fit your paintbrush, and you're ready to go! The handle will allow you to easily carry it around the room and up and down ladders without making a mess.

Opt for "Oops Paint" To save money on painting costs, check out the "Oops Paint" section (yes, that's really what it's called) of your local hardware store. You'll find great deals on brand-new cans of custom paint returned by customers who didn't like the color. It's a great way to find a color for an accent wall or even a primer at a huge discount. You'll pay anywhere from $1 to $5 per can, rather than $20 and up.

Clever Drip Catcher When painting a room directly from the can, it's nearly impossible to keep paint from dripping down the side. So instead of stopping the drips, catch them! The easiest way? Affix a paper or Styrofoam plate to the bottom of the can with some glue or duct tape. That way, it goes with the can wherever you move it, and you can just tear it off when you're done painting.

Who Knew? Classic Tip

Painting doors? Avoid getting paint on the hinges by coating them lightly with petroleum jelly before you start. It's easier to protect the rounded corners than using painter's tape, and it wipes right off!

Get Your Painting Technique Down When painting, instead of wiping the brush on the bucket, tap it on either side. That will allow the excess paint to fall away while still leaving the brushes evenly coated.

Elevate Your Painting Painting a small object on a table? Stick some pushpins into the bottom of the item to elevate it off the table and make it easier to paint. The air will also be able to flow around it as it dries. Then simply remove the pushpins and admire your paint job!

Easy Spray-Painting Spray-painting small items like drawer pulls or knickknacks? Place them in a brown paper bag, then spray paint into the bag and shake it up for a final coating. Dump the items out, and you can throw the bag away with no mess!

Kick Your Baseboards Up a Notch To get the look of bigger baseboards without actually ripping out your old ones, apply a thin piece of molding several inches above where your baseboards end. Then paint the wall space in between the molding and the old baseboard the same color. It's an easy fix that will make a big impact.

An Edgy Solution When painting a windowsill, forget the edging tape: It's expensive, and it can pull up the paint you already have on the sill. So instead, use strips of newspaper. Dampen them and wring out as much excess moisture as you can without ruining the paper, then use them in lieu of tape. They'll stick as long as they're wet, but won't pull up any paint when you're done.

Use Heat to Remove Painter's Tape To be extra careful when removing painter's tape, use a hair dryer over it for a few seconds before pulling it away. It will help loosen the glue so that your new paint job doesn't chip.

Who Knew? Classic Tip

You've been painting baseboards for what seems like hours, thanks to the constant bending over and moving around. Make the job easier on yourself (and your back!) by borrowing your kid's skateboard. It makes a great bench on wheels!

Painting Shortcut When you're done with your paint job, save the leftover paint in case you need to do touch-ups later. The perfect container? A clean shampoo, conditioner, or body-wash container. It will keep away the clutter of old paint cans while keeping the paint fresh. If you need to use some, just dispense it onto a paper plate and get painting!

who knew? THE BIG QUESTION

Leftover Paint

How can I keep leftover paint fresh until I need to use it again? **—Greg Sutton, via Twitter**

Paint Can Balloon The cleverest way we've heard to keep leftover paint from drying up is this crafty maneuver: Blow up a balloon until it's about the size of the remaining space in the can. Then put it inside the can and close the lid. This will reduce the amount of air in the can, thus prolonging the paint's freshness.

Go Upside Down Here's another easy way store leftover paint in the can. First, place a piece of plastic wrap under the paint can's lid, make certain the lid is on tight, and turn the can over. The paint is exposed to less oxygen this way and will last much, much longer.

No Film Method If you hate that film that develops on the top of old paint, you'll love this tip. Before you close the can for storage, place the lid of the can on top of aluminum foil or wax paper and trace around it. Cut out the circle, then drop it gently into the can so it covers the paint. When you open the container later, just take out the foil and you won't have any messy dried paint bits to worry about.

Get Paint Off Glass Accidentally paint the edge of your windowpane while doing some remodeling? Hot vinegar can be used to remove paint from glass. Just microwave a cup of vinegar until hot (about 1 to 2 minutes), then dip a cloth in it and wipe the offending paint away.

For Paint-Covered Hands It's hard not to get paint all over yourself when painting a room. An old household trick is to wipe turpentine on your hands to get latex paint off, but there's a much less smelly way! Simply rub your hands with olive oil, let sit a couple of seconds, then rub off with a damp, soapy sponge. Not only will the olive oil remove the paint, but it's great for your skin, too! For enamel or oil-based paint, rub your hands with wood paste wax, and then wash with soap and water.

Solve a Paint Tray Problem The easiest way to clean a paint tray after you're done rolling on paint is never to get it dirty in the first place! Instead of using plastic wrap or foil, put the paint tray in a plastic bag and pour the paint on top. Once you're done, simply turn the bag inside out and throw away.

See Also . . . For more home-decorating ideas and projects, check out the Easy DIYs chapter.

Wallpaper and Shelf Liners

Got Grease Stains on Your Wall? If grease is still visible on the wall after removing wallpaper, apply a coat of clear varnish to the spots. The grease won't soak through to the new wallpaper.

Who Knew? Classic Tip

Take your wallpaper out of its roll a few days before you hang it and re-roll it the opposite way. It will make it flatter and easier to hang.

Shelf Talk If you're lining shelves in drawers, make sure the contact paper is cut neatly. Place the roll of liner in an empty box of wax paper, plastic wrap, or aluminum foil, and simply tear off the amount you need. You'll have a much straighter line than if you had used scissors.

Smoother Shelf Liners To make shelf paper easier to apply, stick it in the freezer for 30 to 45 minutes. The paper will be a little firmer and less likely to leave behind bubbles and bumps when you stick it on the shelf.

A Better Fix for Wallpaper If your wallpaper needs a fix-up in a small area, don't use scissors to cut off the replacement piece. Instead, tear it off with your hands. The ragged edge of the new piece will blend in better than a straight edge.

Plumbing and Pipes

Fix a Running Toilet with a Straw If your toilet runs for a long time after each flush, you're wasting water! If the problem is that valve gets stuck open when the flapper chain gets tangled, here's an easy fix: Simply cut a straw so it's about 6 inches long, then thread the chain through it. It will keep the chain from tangling.

Ditch the Drano If your drain is starting to run a little slow, but doesn't require a heavy-duty drain declogger like Drano, save your pipes the wear and tear by using dishwashing liquid instead. Just squirt a good amount of dishwashing soap in the drain and let it sit for 15 minutes. Then boil a kettle of water, and pour it down the drain. The soap will break up the grease, and the hot water will wash it away.

Surprising Declogger Kitchen sink clogged up? Here's another way you can get it clear without commercial drain cleaners, which contain harsh chemicals that can destroy your pipes. Instead, slip three Alka-Seltzer tablets down the drain and turn on the hot water for just a few seconds. The tablets will fizz up and get to work on the clog. After 15 minutes, run the water again and the drain should be clog-free.

Who Knew? Classic Tip

Does your toilet tank have a leak? To find out, put a drop of food coloring in the tank and see if it shows up in the bowl. If it does, fix the leak to save up to 73,000 gallons of water per year!

A Pain in the Drain Make sure to drain your water heater once a year to get rid of sediment. Left too long, this grit can build up until you're using energy to heat sludge. To find out how to complete this simple home maintenance trick, type "how to drain a water heater" into Google or another search engine. And start to save!

Keep Sprayers from Snarling Do you have to jiggle your kitchen sink's sprayer hose loose every time you want to use it? The hose is probably catching on the shutoff valves below. To keep it moving effortlessly, simply slip ½ inch foam pipe insulation over the water pipes and shutoff handles in the cabinet below your sink. The piping costs less than $3 at home supply stores!

Who Knew? Classic Tip

Instead of using expensive Teflon tape to prevent leaking between pipes and other parts that screw together, just use dental floss. Wrap the floss around the item's threads, and you'll have a tight connection.

Outdoor Projects

Awesome Autumnal Helper Never pay to have your gutters cleaned again! To easily keep falling leaves from clogging them up, place a Slinky (yes, the child's toy) in your gutters. Stretch it out, then fasten the ends to your gutters with binder clips. The coil will allow water to get through, but keep leaves out.

Removing Shifty Shingles Notice a shingle that's cracked or curled? Or maybe you're ready for a complete re-siding or re-roofing project. To remove shingles without breaking your back (and wrists), use a shovel with a square head. Starting at the bottom of a tile, squeeze the edge of your shovel underneath and pry open the space between the shingle and the roof or wall. Lift up and the shingle will pop off.

Who Knew? Classic Tip

If one of your roof's shingles has fallen off, you can make a temporary replacement using duct tape. Cut a ¼-inch-thick piece of plywood to match the same size as the missing shingle. Then wrap it in duct tape (you will need several strips), and wedge it in place. Use extra duct tape to keep it there, if necessary.

Perfectly Painted Fence If you've ever painted a fence, you know that the task can be onerous, and you can end up dripping paint all over your lawn. Protect the grass by placing an old dustpan under the section you're working on. It will catch spills and help prevent you from picking up pieces of dirt and grass on your paintbrush. If you don't want paint splatters on your dustpan, cover it with newspaper first.

Guard Outdoor Light Bulbs from Winter Wear Before it gets too cold, consider applying a thin layer of petroleum jelly to the threads of all your outdoor light bulbs. It will prevent them from rusting and make them easier to replace when they blow out.

Snow Shoveling Made Easy Here's a tip that those of you who live in snowy climates will appreciate. Before going out to shovel snow, coat the blade of your snow shovel with cooking spray. That way the snow and ice will slide right off the shovel instead of sticking to it. This works on both plastic and metal shovels.

See Also . . . For more tips on outdoor areas, check out the Perfecting Your Garden and Yard chapter.

For the Garage Floor Are there nasty oil stains on your concrete garage floor? Just pour on some paint thinner on them, then cover with kitty litter. Let sit for 30 minutes (with the garage door open), then you can simply sweep it all up.

chapter 3

Car Mechanics' Secrets

Auto Answers

Maintenance Matters

Easy Repairs

Cleaning Your Car

Car Interior Solutions

Cold Weather Tips

Auto Answers

What's the Frequency? Want to know how to increase the range of your car's keyless entry by 30 percent? Just press it against your head as you use it. It will conduct the (perfectly safe) radio signal through your body, giving its travel power a boost. Strange but true!

Rescue Your Remote When your car's keyless remote needs a new battery, don't head to the dealership for a replacement—depending on the kind of car you have, it can cost anywhere from $50 to $150. Instead, pry open your remote and check the size and type of battery you need. Then head to a hardware or electronics store for a much cheaper alternative.

When It's Cheaper to Run the AC Roll up your windows on the highway. Having the wind streaming through your hair might be fun, but it increases drag on the car and takes more energy to run. In this case, it's actually usually cheaper to run the AC.

Car-Maintenance Myth Many new car owners believe that in order to maintain their car's warranty, all maintenance and repairs must be done at the dealership—where prices are at a premium. Not true! As long as you use the manufacturer's recommended parts and fluids, keep good records, and hang on to all your receipts, you can take the car to whichever mechanic you prefer, which can often save you a ton of cash.

Who Knew? Classic Tip

If you are waiting for longer than 30 seconds in your car, turn off the engine. You use more fuel idling after 30 seconds than you use to restart your car.

Parking Know-How Backing into a parking spot so you're ready to just simply drive out when you restart your car isn't just a way to show off—it can save energy. Getting the car into a spot takes more energy than driving because you're moving the car into the different gears, as well as starting and stopping. Having the car do this work at the end of a drive rather than at the beginning of one saves energy because at the end of a drive your car's engine is already warm.

Keep It Shady One of the easiest ways to save on fuel costs for your car is to park in the shade on summer days!

who knew? THE BIG QUESTION

Saving at the Pump

Nice tips for saving gas once it's in your car. But do you have any tips on spending less at the pump? **—Qia Williams, via WhoKnewTips.com**

The Easy Route to Cheap Gas The best and easiest way to spend less at the pump is to visit GasBuddy.com first. Enter your zip code, and your new buddy will tell you the nearby gas stations with the lowest prices. You can also search to find the least expensive pump prices in your entire city or state. They even have cell-phone apps!

Go the Distance When you're on the highway and it's time to fill up on gas, drive a little farther off the highway exit before choosing a station. The gas stations closest to the highway will often charge more per gallon than the ones located a bit off your course—you could save a few bucks by going the extra distance.

Wait Till Tuesday or Wednesday The cheapest time to refuel your car is on Tuesday and Wednesday. People fuel up on Thursdays and Fridays for weekend trips, and on Monday for their workweek. Therefore, most gas stations do their weekly price changes on Tuesdays or Wednesdays.

Stick with Regular Did you know that only 5 percent of cars run better on premium gas as opposed to regular? Make sure to check your owner's manual to see what it recommends.

The air-conditioning is one of the most fuel-draining parts of your car. Having to cool your car back down to a non-sweltering temperature uses a lot more gas than you might think! Also, make sure to invest in a sun-blocking windshield shade if you do have to park in a hot spot.

Time for a Change? Like a good car owner, you just checked your car's oil and noticed that the dipstick is black. Does it mean that you need an oil change stat? Not necessarily. Oil can darken with use, so check your owner's manual. Most newer cars only need an oil change every 7,500 miles or so (or about once or twice a year).

Start Your Engines If you have a newer car, you can skip the long warm-ups, even in winter! Today's cars are designed to warm up while being driven, so after you give the car 30 to 60 seconds of idling time, you can be on your way—just take it easy for the first few minutes on the road. You'll save both time and gas!

Save the Mitts When it's time to retire your oven mitts because they're covered in stains and burn marks, don't throw them away. Save them for use with your car. Oven mitts are great when handling hot engine parts or even as a washing mitt.

Maintenance Matters

Pristine Car Batteries Accumulated dirt and corrosion on your battery terminal can interfere with its performance, especially in the winter when debris may mean you can't start your car. Baking soda is all you need to keep the terminal clean. Combine water and baking soda into a paste and make sure your car is turned off before you open the hood. Scrub the battery with the paste and wipe down with a clean rag.

Who Knew? Classic Tip

You should always fill up your gas tank before it dips below a quarter of a tank. Having a sufficient amount of fuel will ensure your car's fuel injection system stays healthy.

Don't Tread on Me Does your car need new tires? To find out, put Abe Lincoln to work. Place a penny in your tire's shallowest tread, with Abe facing the hubcap. If you can see the hair on top of the president's head, the tread is worn down to the point that you should buy new tires.

O_2 and Your Car When your car's oxygen sensors start to degrade, your fuel efficiency can decrease by up to 15 percent. Given the high cost of fuel, it makes sense to replace them before the "check engine" light even has a chance to turn on. Newer vehicles need new oxygen sensors every 100,000 miles, while those built before 1996 should be changed every 60,000 miles. Check your owner's manual to be certain when yours need to be replaced, and save!

Who Knew? Classic Tip

To prevent your car's battery from corroding, wipe down the battery posts with petroleum jelly once every couple of months.

Spark It Up Did you know that you can save money by changing your spark plugs 20,000 miles earlier than the car's manufacturer recommends? The misfires and incomplete combustion that happen during those last 20,000 miles can actually cost you hundreds of dollars in lost fuel. Most manufacturers recommend you change the spark plugs at 100,000 miles, but you should try to change them closer to 80,000 miles instead. (Check your owner's manual to see what your car's manufacturer recommends.)

Oil Change Options When it comes to getting an oil change, synthetic oil may seem like the more expensive option, but it may actually save you money in the long run. Synthetic motor oil is cleaner and lubricates moving parts better, meaning it can extend your car's life, especially in cold weather. In many cars, you can even go longer between oil changes. Ask your auto mechanic for more information.

Easy Repairs

Chrome Polish Need a chrome polish? It's as simple as vinegar. Apply directly on chrome with a rag for a quick, simple shine.

Let the Mechanic Come to You For small repairs to the body of your car, like fixing dents and scrapes, consider using a mobile repair service such as YourMechanic.com. They'll come right to you, and they're often much cheaper—and faster—than a body shop.

Save on Touch-Ups Here's a tip that can save you big money on fixing nicks and scratches on your car. Instead of paying $100 or more for touch-up work at a detail shop, keep some touch-up paint around. Go to AutomotiveTouchup.com (or back to the dealership) with your car's VIN number, and they can provide you with the exact paint match for much less. You can often get it in spray-paint form, which is so easy to apply you won't even be able to tell it was done in your driveway. Plus, you'll have the extra paint at the ready for the next time your car gets an annoying scratch.

Who Knew? Classic Tip

If your car battery has died and you don't have jumper cables, don't get a headache just yet. First, try dropping a couple of aspirin tablets into the battery. The acid in the aspirin can provide it with just enough charge to get you to the nearest service station.

Get Free Installations! It's not widely known, but many chain autoparts stores like Pep Boys and Advanced Auto Parts will do simple installations for free if you buy the parts at their store! You could save $20 to $30 or more in labor costs on windshield wipers, batteries, taillights, and other items. Be sure to ask about this service at the customer service counter or call ahead to make sure your local store participates.

Plunge a Car Dent Believe it or not, there may be a way to remove that dent from the side of your car without spending a penny. Rub petroleum jelly on the edge of a clean toilet plunger, then place it over the dent and pump it out just like you would a toilet clog! Your family will laugh at you until the dent pops out and you save a $300 trip to the mechanic!

Tire Trick You suspect your car has a hole in its tire, but you can't figure out where. Use this trick to locate the leak and patch it up: Fill a spray bottle with water and a few squirts of dishwashing liquid. Spray all over your tire in bright light and look carefully for a cluster of air bubbles. They'll point the way to the tiny hole in your tire.

Cleaning Your Car

Windshield Bugs Be Gone! Not only are smooshed bugs on your windshield gross to look at, they can be very difficult to wash off—your wipers only spread the gunk and, once the bugs dry and harden, they become so stuck on that they need to be scraped off. However, we have an easy removal solution! The next time your windshield and headlights are splattered with bug guts, apply a generous amount of hydrogen peroxide to the stains and let sit. After a couple minutes, apply peroxide to a paper towel and wipe the gunky spots, which should come off easily, and then wash your car as usual.

Tar on Your Car? It's easy to remove tar from your car's exterior. Make a paste of baking soda and water, then apply it to the tar with a soft cloth. Let it dry, then rinse off with warm water.

Who Knew? Classic Tip

Tree sap dripping on your car is one of the hazards of summer, but you can remove it easily with butter or margarine. Just rub the butter onto the sap with a soft cloth, and it comes right off.

Bumper Sticker Remover If it's finally time to remove that bumper sticker from the last election from your car, use hand sanitizer to make the job easier. Rub it into the sticker and let sit for 15 minutes. It will help dissolve the glue and will practically wipe right off!

Cleaning Off Brake Dust To remove brake dust—that fine, black powder—from your car's tires, apply a bit of cooking spray or vegetable oil, let sit for 10 minutes, and wipe off. Then spray them again when you're done. The vegetable oil will reduce the collection of dust in the future, and you'll be able to wipe it off even more easily next time.

Wheel Washer Cleaning hubcaps and wheel covers can take "getting your hands dirty" to another level. Ditch the elbow grease by sticking these tire parts in the dishwasher instead (but do not place actual dishes in the same load!). Turn the machine to the pots-and-pans wash cycle to get your wheels sparkling clean.

Who Knew? Classic Tip

Messy windshield wipers are a safety hazard, and they're also pretty annoying. If your wipers are smearing the windows, wipe the blades with some rubbing alcohol.

Sweep the Ceiling The next time you vacuum the car, don't forget about the ceiling! Smoke and other smells can collect there, so give it a good cleaning as well. You'll find that your car stays fresher for longer afterward!

Car Interior Solutions

Safeguard Tissue Boxes If you're like us, you keep a box of tissues in the car to clean up sniffles and other inevitable spills that happen on the road. To make sure your car's tissue box doesn't get flattened by bumps on the road and the feet of restless children, make a plastic cover out of a leftovers container! Get a reusable plastic container like Glad-Ware that fits the size of the tissue box ("potluck" size works well). Then cut a rectangular strip out of the bottom center of the container—this will be the slit you'll pull the Kleenex out of. Place the box of tissues upside-down inside the container, so the opening of the tissue box aligns with the strip you just cut out. Cover with the lid, and turn it right-side up. You should be able to pull tissues from the open slot, and your cardboard box is road-safe.

Cute Car Freshener Here's a way to personalize your car and make it smell delicious. Find an image you like online, make two printouts, and cut them out. Next, glue each printout to an empty cereal box and cut out around each shape again, so you have two cardboard-backed images. Now take a new dish sponge and cut it out in the same shape. Glue one image to each side of the sponge with superglue. Next, use a needle to thread a string through the top of the sponge and tie it in a loop. Finally, squeeze about 10 drops of your favorite essential oil onto the sponge and hang in the car. The best part is you can just add a few more drops of essential oil when the scent starts to fade!

Who Knew? Classic Tip

Oh no, your kids tore a hole in your car's seat. (OK, so it wasn't the kids, it was you.) Instead of getting an expensive upholstery replacement, use an iron-on patch instead. Hold the patch in place with a few straight pins while you iron. If you don't have a long enough extension cord to bring the iron into your car, set the iron on one setting higher than the directions on the patch recommend. When it heats up, unplug it and quickly bring it out to the car.

Repurpose a Backpack Your daughter is suddenly too cool for her Dora the Explorer backpack. It's not even worn out, but it's not really your look, either. A great way to repurpose it is to use it as storage in your car! It will easily hang on the back of one of the front seats, and keep all those odds in ends that usually litter the floor.

Free Floor Mats If your car's floor mats need to be replaced, consider going to a carpet store and finding some samples to use instead. You'll always be able to find samples that are gray or another color to match your car's interior, and best of all, they're free!

Who Knew? Classic Tip

Sick of things rattling around your truck bed? Divide it into several compartments for storage by using spring-loaded shower curtain rods. Brace the rods against the sides of your truck bed and each other. They'll keep larger items from shifting during your drive.

Cloves in the Car Do you hate the smell of store-bought car air fresheners? An easy and great-smelling substitute is to simply take a handful of cloves and put them in your car's ashtrays or cup holders. The sweet scent will freshen up your car in no time—for pennies!

No More Trunk Thumping Rubberized shelf liners can be just as useful in your car's trunk as in your cabinets. Lay them down over the bottom of your trunk and the items inside will be less likely to move around while you're driving.

Repurposed Car Storage An empty baby-wipes container can be put to great use in your car—as a handy travel kit! Inside, store a first-aid kit, tissues, cough drops, small toys for the kids, or anything else you've wished you had in your car for long trips.

Turn a Visor into an Organizer Turn your car's visor into a handy place to store paper and other flat items by using rubber bands. Wrap several rubber bands snugly around the visor, then slip papers, CDs, or anything else under the rubber bands.

Cold Weather Tips

Dry De-Icer In our house nothing says bad mood faster than a frozen driveway during the morning rush and rock salt that's all clumped together and impossible to separate. You might be powerless against frozen driveways and walkways, but you can keep them safe by having your rock salt ready to go. Charcoal briquettes will collect extra moisture in the bag to prevent clumping. Just drop a few briquettes in with the rock salt and you'll be ready for the first storm.

who knew? THE BIG QUESTION

Keeping Ice Away

I spent way too much time trying to get the ice off my car this morning. Any hints?

—Donna Grant McDougall, via Facebook

Preventing Ice Before It Starts Make your morning routine with your car a little easier with a saltwater solution! Wiping saltwater on your windshield, windows, and mirrors before you go to bed will ensure that ice doesn't form on them overnight. Now you can sleep in an extra five minutes, at least!

Save Time on Mirrors and Wipers Save yourself scraping and wiping time each morning by wrapping your side mirrors and windshield wipers in old plastic bags. Then just remove them and you're on your way!

No More Windshield Ice When the forecast calls for ice or snow, protect your car by placing two old bath towels across your windshield. When it's time to drive, simply pull off the towels and you're ready to go.

Quickly Remove Ice Ice covering your windshield and you're not making much headway with the ice scraper? Pour, rub, or spray the windshield with a mixture of half lukewarm water and half rubbing alcohol. The frost will easily melt away. (Never pour hot water on your windshield. The glass may expand from the heat and then contract as it cools, causing the windshield to crack.)

Ice Ice Baby Powder Car doors inevitably freeze shut on the days you are already late, but they don't have to. Use baby powder or baking soda to absorb the moisture that collects on the rubber-seal lining of your car door. Just wipe the weather strip with a dry cloth before sprinkling on the powder. Repeat every few days in the dead of winter to make sure you can always get into your car.

Handy Ice Scraper Empty CD jewel cases always seem to be lying around when you don't need them—but here's one time you might. If you can't find your ice scraper one morning, grab a jewel case and scrape away to get those frosty winter windows clear.

Who Knew? Classic Tip

If your car gets stuck in an icy patch and your wheels aren't getting any traction, help free it by using your car's floor mats. Take them out and place under the tires, then drive to a safe place, retrieve the mats, and be on your way.

Wax on . . . Your Headlights Car wax may strike some as a vanity, but in winter it's important for safety. Layers of salt and slush on the roads leave debris on your car's headlights that compromise their effectiveness. Keep them in working order by cleaning and coating them with car wax. Repeat monthly as needed.

Stop Ice Before It Starts To keep your car's door locks safe from ice during the cold winter months, place a refrigerator magnet over the lock. You can even take an old magnet (last year's calendar from a local realtor, perhaps) and cut it into pieces that fit perfectly, protecting the keyholes from ice.

Spring for the Seat Warmers Heated seats in your car may seem like a luxury, but they can actually be a huge money-saver. Heated seats don't have to use as much energy as your car's heating vents to keep you warm. If they aren't offered when you buy your car, consider getting a heated pad for your seat or even having heated seats installed after-market.

Impromptu Shovel Stuck in the snow (or mud) with no way to dig yourself out? A shovel may be closer than you think. Just remove your hubcap and use it instead.

chapter 4

Perfecting Your Garden and Yard

Make Yard Work Easier

Keeping Your Garden Healthy

Practically Free Fertilizers

Sprouting Every Seed

Pruning Pointers

Attracting Fauna

Cleaning Outdoor Areas

Make Yard Work Easier

When to Water Plants Did you know that the best time to water your plants is in the morning? At that time, the roots will be able to absorb the most water, making sure your greens stay refreshed longer.

Who Knew? Classic Tip

Good for you for remembering to water your garden! Just make sure you're not overdoing it. Here's a simple test. When you're finished with the hose, dig down half a foot or so and feel the soil. Moist is fine, but muddy means you should use a lighter hand.

Free Kneepads Rather than buy gardening kneepads at the store, make your own with items that usually find their way to the recycling bin. Fold newspaper into a square several inches across and about an inch thick, then tape to secure. Then place the square into a plastic grocery bag, wrap tightly, and tape shut with packing or duct tape. You can even duct tape them to jeans! Now you have gardening kneepads and you didn't spend a cent.

Foiled Again It always seems so wasteful to throw away barely used pieces of aluminum foil. Here is a great way to reuse scraps. Store cleaned foil with your garden supplies, and use the crumpled up balls to scrub mud off of your tools.

Who Knew? Classic Tip

Don't just toss your garden tools in a bin or bucket when you're done with them; they'll eventually rust. To prevent this, submerge the metal parts in a bucket of sand whenever the tools are not in use. (Better yet, add some mineral oil to the sand.) Make sure the sand is stored in a dry place where rainwater can't get into it, though. If you decide you don't want to store your tools in sand, another option is to toss a handful of tea leaves in whatever container you keep them in. The antioxidants in tea react with iron and form a protective film that will help keep the metal nice, new, and rust-free.

Brown Lawn? If your grass turns brown after mowing, either you've cut it too short or the lawn mower blades are dull. Dull blades tear up the grass instead of clipping it cleanly. It may be time for a new mower.

who knew? THE BIG QUESTION

Watering with a Hose

I feel like I go through a new hose every other summer. Any ideas for what to do with the old hose other than just throwing it away?

—Dianne Harlow, via Facebook

Easy Fix for a Hose with Holes It may drive you crazy to hear your kids chomping away on gum but when it comes to a small leak in your hose, gum will actually serve you. To minimize the "ick" factor you may want to chew on a new piece yourself. Cover the hole with gum and massage it outward so it extends ½ inch in any direction. It will harden by the next day and last over a month!

Make a Soaker Hose If you can't beat 'em, join 'em. One thing you can do with an old, holey hose is to simply repurpose it as a soaker hose. It's easy: Just poke some more holes in your hose along its length with a straight pen, then place in your garden to slowly water your plants.

Store Your Hose Properly To make your hose last longer to begin with, store it coiled, rather than folded. Try coiling it around a bucket!

One Final Re-Use If your hose is truly a goner, here's a way you can give it a new use around your home. Cut off a length of the hose, then cut a slit through it. It will make the perfect cover for ice skate blades, a saw, or another sharp item.

Protect Your Plants While Watering When watering your garden with a hose, take care not to drag the hose over your plants. Place a few short, heavy stakes in your garden to create an alleyway for the hose, restraining it from rolling around and distressing the delicate plants. If you don't have stakes, simply cut a wire hanger into 6-inch pieces, bend them into arches, and use them to guide your hose.

Who Knew? Classic Tip

The rain stopped just in time for your outdoor party, but not in enough time for the grass to dry before you want to mow it. To solve this problem, simply spray the blades of your lawnmower with vegetable oil or nonstick cooking spray, and the grass won't stick!

Easy Irrigation System Creating a slow-drip irrigation system in your garden is as easy as saving some plastic soda bottles! This subterranean watering system will help your garden thrive since the gradual, continuous flow of water starts at the roots—and it's less time you'll spend watering! Rinse out a 2-liter plastic bottle, then cut a couple slits at the bottom and two more slits at the sides using a knife or screwdriver. Test the drip holes by pouring water into the bottle; the drips should be slow and steady. Now dig a hole in your garden next to the plants you'd like to water, and insert the bottle so that only the top few inches are exposed. Fill the bottle with water every few days if it hasn't rained. The bottle will deliver slow-release moisture to the roots, right where the plant needs it. You can also use this technique to water indoor plants while you're on vacation!

Keeping Your Garden Healthy

Coal for Your Soil When you break out the charcoal for grilling season, save a few briquettes for your garden. Crush them into pieces about 1-inch wide and sprinkle them on top of the soil. Not only is the carbon in the charcoal great for plants, but the charcoal also absorbs water and then slowly releases it, meaning that your plants' roots will stay moister for longer.

Get to the Roots Help strengthen your plant's root system with hydrogen peroxide—the extra pump of oxygen from the peroxide prevents root rot and over-watering. Just mix a tablespoon of hydrogen peroxide with 2 cups water, and water your plant with the solution. Its disinfectant properties will fend off bacteria, mold, fungus, and other nasty soil-borne diseases.

Increase Soil Acidity If you live in a hard-water area, add 1 cup vinegar to 1 gallon water, then use it to water plants that love acidic soil, such as rhododendrons, heather, and azaleas. The vinegar will release iron in the soil for the plants to use.

Who Knew? Classic Tip

If you have smaller outdoor plants, you don't necessarily need to bring them inside to keep them protected from frost. Simply cover them at night with small plastic garbage bags (the kind that have pull handles), and tie the handles snugly around the pots. Don't forget to remove the bags in the morning, though, so the plants can soak up the sun.

Plant Doctor A broken stem doesn't have to mean the end of a flower. If you catch it in time, you can save the limb by making a little splint out of a toothpick and tape. It looks a little funny, but your kids will get a kick out of it, and it makes a great lesson in resilience.

who knew? THE BIG QUESTION

Removing Weeds

Any tips for easy ways to get rid of weeds?

—Luke Ambrose, via Facebook

Wait for Rain We hate weeding too! One thing to remember is that weeding is easier when the plants are wet. Save this dull task for post-rain or watering. When you give a yank, it will be easier to get the whole plant out at the root.

Hammer Help Using a hammer is an easy way to make weeding quicker. Kneel down, turn the hammer backward, and bang it onto the soil to catch the weed between the claw. Now just pull!

Viva Vinegar! You can keep sidewalks or other paved areas of your yard looking spiffy with this trick. To remove weeds from sidewalk and driveway cracks, pour vinegar straight from the bottle onto the weed. It will die within a few days.

Easy Weed Prevention Stop weeds before they start with this simple trick: Wet newspapers and layer them around your plants (then cover with dirt and mulch so your yard doesn't look like a recycling bin!). The newspaper will keep the weeds away from the sun so they never even start growing!

Let Your Lawn Grow To keep weeds out of your lawn, try to keep the grass about three inches high. The higher the lawn, the less direct sunlight is available for pesky weeds to grow.

Reviving Plants This may sound like a cure from the Middle Ages, but garlic does a fine job of reviving diseased plants. Grate two cloves into 4 cups water and use as much as you need to quench the thirst of your struggling plants. Given the myriad health benefits garlic offers to humans, it's not surprising it can help the immobile organisms that share your home (and we don't mean your spouse and kids).

A Fungus Among Us To kill fungus on your plants, brew up an extra-strong cup of chamomile tea, and spray the cooled tea all over the leaves. Repeat daily until the fungus is gone.

Cinnamon Spray for Plants Cinnamon is another great natural fungicide for plants and the soil. To use, combine 1 teaspoon ground cinnamon with 1 quart water in a spray bottle. Spray wherever you see the fungus, and repeat every 10 days to keep fungus away for good.

See Also . . . For all-natural ways to get rid of bugs and other pests that are eating your plants, consult the All-Natural Pest Repellents chapter.

Practically Free Fertilizers

Back to the Land Cereal crumbs are a drag in your cereal bowl but they're great for plants, supplying much-needed nutrients to the soil, which makes sense given that they're grains that came from the soil in the first place! Instead of shaking the box over the trash before ripping it up for recycling, dump the remains of the flakes into your house-plants or garden for a treat they'll love.

Easy Nitrogen for Plants Plants love nitrogen, but you don't have to pay top dollar for fertilizers that have nitrogen in them. To make your own slow-release, nitrogen-rich fertilizer, dissolve a packet of unflavored gelatin in 3 cups warm water. Then use it to water plants in need of a little TLC. You'll get all the benefits of an expensive fertilizer without the price tag!

Make Your Own Bonemeal As you may know, bonemeal is an excellent source of nutrients for your plants. But instead of spending $8 to $10 on a bag at your local gardening store, make your own! Bonemeal is just bones, after all. Save bones from chicken, turkey, steaks, and stews, then dry them out by roasting them in a 425°F oven for a half an hour or microwaving them on high for

1 to 6 minutes (depending on how many bones you have). Place them in a plastic or paper bag and grind them up by hitting them with a hammer then rolling them with a rolling pin. Mix the resulting powder into your soil for a life-producing treat for your plants. And you didn't spend a cent!

Who Knew? Classic Tip

This advice definitely sounds like an urban legend, but it's such an easy way to grow fantastic, sweet peppers that you have to try it. A matchbook buried with each pepper plant will transmit sulfur, a great fertilizer for them. In addition, to give these nutrient-seeking plants the magnesium they need, add 2 tablespoons Epsom salts to ½ gallon water and soak the plants with the mixture when you see the first blossoms of the year.

Banana Boost Mix dried banana peels in with the soil next time you plant something new; you'll give it the potassium and phosphorous it needs to grow beautifully.

Shake on the Fertilizer Here's a great second use for an old grated Parmesan cheese container. Fill the empty container with granular fertilizer and shake it on your garden.

The shaker's holes are a perfect size for distributing the necessary nutrients to your plants without overfertilizing.

Sprouting Every Seed

Old News You Can Use Instead of buying fiber seed-starting pots, try making your own—for free!—with old newspapers. It takes a bit of work, but they'll be as good as store-bought and you won't spend a cent. First, shred some newspaper, either in a paper shredder or by hand, and place it in a bucket with water to cover. The next day, put this mixture in a food processor or blender, and blend well. (You will probably need to work in batches.) Squeeze out the excess water with your hands or through a rag, and then press the newspaper pulp into a muffin tin. Place the tin in the sun or in the oven on the lowest heat setting available. Allow the mixture to dry completely before removing from the tin. Your seed-starters are ready to use!

Sprout Support Keep a bottle of hydrogen peroxide handy for your garden! Peroxide's antibacterial, antifungal, and antiviral properties will completely sterilize your seeds, boosting their germinating powers. Before you start to germinate the seeds in the spring, soak them in a solution of 2 teaspoons hydrogen peroxide for every 1 cup water. Soak your seeds for 24 hours, or up to 48 hours for hard seeds. Add more peroxide solution as necessary to keep the seeds moist throughout their soak time.

Freezing Seeds If you have more seeds than you can use this spring, store them in a sealed container in your freezer. The cold will keep them fresh until next year.

Who Knew? Classic Tip

If a scarecrow doesn't work to keep birds from feasting on your grass seeds, try this modern-day equivalent before you resort to netting. Place stakes at the four corners of the area you want to protect. Now cut two pieces of string, long enough to reach diagonally in an X across the lawn. Every foot or two along the strings you'll want to tie 1-inch strips of aluminum foil. The breeze will keep the aluminum pieces flapping about and will scare off would-be invaders.

When Does Your Garden Grow? Not sure when is the best month to plant vegetables in your area? Check out SproutRobot.com. Enter your zip code, and it will tell you when to start seeds, when to transplant seedlings, and even how to grow everything from Asian greens to zucchini and everything in between!

Go Deep When you plant seeds, you want to make sure you bury them at the correct depth. Save time and energy by marking 1-inch measurements on the handles of your tools instead of using a ruler.

Who Knew? Classic Tip

Not sure which seed you planted where? Write the name of the plant on a plastic knife and shove it into the ground nearby.

Help from a Hose Here's a great tip if you have trouble planting your garden in neat rows. Run a hose in a straight line along the ground, then plant your new seedlings along the hose. Remove the hose and you'll have a perfect-looking flowerbed!

Garden Tea Party Did you know that watering your plants with tea every now and then is good for them, because it supplies them with tannic acid and nutrients that help them grow? Because of this, using tea bags when planting new grass can be your secret to success. Wet the bags then lay them in the dirt to make an inviting "bed" for the grass seeds. Then sprinkle on the seeds and water frequently.

Pruning Pointers

Pinch Protector Keep clothespins on hand when you are pruning your bushes to keep branches out of your way. (Think of hairdressers clipping parts of your hair up while they are working on other sections.) The clothespins also allow you to grip the thorny branches of rose bushes, raspberries, or thistles without risk of injury, whereas thorns often poke through gardening gloves.

Who Knew? Classic Tip

Use a solution of bleach and water to disinfect pruning shears after you're done so you don't spread diseases between plants. Rinse with tepid water until the bleach is gone.

Tree Sculpting Pruning will be less of a chore if you keep your eye on the goal of a strong and healthy tree. If it's more of a motivator, though, remember you don't want to get sued if a weak branch falls on a neighbor. On pruning day, follow a simple plan: First get rid of any branches that are clearly dead, dying, or infested. Then home in on the ones that are too long, crisscrossing each other, or growing weak. Step back and admire your work.

Attracting Fauna

Bring Butterflies to Your Backyard Who doesn't love watching butterflies glide around in their backyard? Whip up this nutritious food to welcome more beautiful butterflies into your lives: Combine 1 pound sugar, 1 cup fruit juice, 1 cup molasses or syrup, 1 to 2 cans stale beer, 1 shot rum, and 3 mashed overripe bananas. Mix well and spray onto surfaces around your yard—try fences, trees, or rocks. Your neighbors might think you're strange, but the butterflies will love it!

Orange Bird Feeders Attract more birds to your backyard with these orange-half feeders. Cut an orange in half, and scoop out all of the pulp. With an awl, make four evenly spaced holes along the edge of each empty half. Then hang it from a tree by running yarn through the holes and tying to a tree branch, open side up. Fill with birdseed, and enjoy watching your new avian friends. This is also a great activity to do with kids!

Farm-Fresh Birdseed The bottom of a paper egg carton makes a handy little bird feeder. Paint it if you'd like, then punch holes in the corners and use string to attach it to a tree branch. Each section can hold a little birdseed.

Who Knew? Classic Tip

Want to make your birdbath a hot spot for your feathered friends? Simply add some colorful marbles or pebbles to attract neighborhood birds. The brighter the color, the better!

Peanut Butter Is for the Birds! Our kids love seeing birds swoop into the backyard for feeding time. Here's another easy way to make homemade bird feeders: All you'll need is an empty toilet paper roll, birdseed, and peanut butter. Spread peanut butter all around the surface of the roll. Pour birdseed onto a paper plate, then roll the sticky cardboard in it until it's covered completely in seeds. Slip the bird feeder onto a tree branch, and watch as new feathered friends stop by for a snack!

Cleaning Outdoor Areas

Mind Your Mildew If your deck is covered with mildew, try spraying the wood with straight vinegar. Leave it for an hour or so, then rinse off. The acid in the vinegar kills mold and mildew, and will help get your deck clean. Another option is to use hydrogen peroxide: Spray on, let sit for 30 minutes, then rinse.

Easy Trashcan Clean The outdoor trashcan is one of the grossest spots to clean. However, the chore will be a little less nasty if you try this simple trick: Use a drill to make a few ½-inch holes in the bottom of the pail. Now you can shoot a hose inside for a quick wash, rather than dumping out filthy water every time you clean it. The holes also allow rainwater to drain out on its own.

The Easiest Clean Pool Who knew the easiest way to clean your pool was with some tennis balls? Simply throw a couple of clean tennis balls into your pool, and their fabric will soak up oils on the surface of the water caused by bodies, sunscreen, and dirt. Take them out of the pool and clean them, then put them back in every few times you use the pool and it will stay clean all summer!

who knew? THE BIG QUESTION

Cleaning Outdoor Furniture

My mother's porch furniture has seen better days, but she can't afford to replace it right now. Are there any ways to make it look better?

—Maria Velez, via Facebook

Wicker Wonder We'll get your mom's patio looking like new again! If it's wicker or plastic, first vacuum up the freestanding dirt on the seat and arms. Then cover the whole piece with a mixture of 1 gallon warm water and 3 tablespoons ammonia. Scrub it with a brush to get between the fibers, then let it dry.

Renew Wood To bring the life back into wooden patio furniture, rub vegetable oil or cooking spray over the clean furniture to revitalize the dried-out wood. Buff with a dry cloth for extra polish.

Patio Furniture Quick Clean The laziest way to clean plastic or resin patio furniture? Just toss it in the swimming pool before going to bed, and in the morning it'll be good as new. Meanwhile, your pool's filter will clean up the dirt.

Don't Mess with Mold If mold or mildew is the issue, it's vinegar to the rescue. Spray or rub white vinegar directly onto patio and lawn furniture. Let it sit for a few hours before wiping down with a damp cloth.

Don't Let Your Driveway Go to the Dogs For some reason, all the dogs in the neighborhood seem to think your driveway is the perfect place to mark their territory. Neutralize the odor by mixing together 7 cups vinegar, 7 cups water, and 1 cup baking soda. Saturate the area with the solution, allow it to dry, then hose it off. The neighborhood dogs will find some other place to relieve themselves.

Who Knew? Classic Tip

If you have stains on paving stones or a concrete patio, sometimes the solution is simple. Try pouring hot water from several feet above the stone onto the stain. Repeat several times, and your stain may just disappear. If this doesn't work, try rubbing some dishwashing liquid into the spot with a toothbrush, then rinsing off. For really tough stains, add a bit of ammonia to the water.

Vinyl Siding Super-Cleaner We use baking soda to clean all over our home—even on the outside! From bird poop to tree sap to standard weather damage, vinyl siding can get very dirty. And while brand-name cleaners will no doubt get the job done, they tend to be costly and loaded with toxic chemicals. Happily, you can save yourself a run to the hardware store by making your own siding cleaner with one of our favorite household helpers: baking soda. Combine baking soda with enough water to form a paste, then scrub into your siding with a damp rag until the stains lift. Rinse off with a hose and, if necessary, repeat on stubborn stains.

Algae Antidote Your birdbath used to be a hot spot for the feathered folk, but ever since it became slimy with algae, they've stayed away! Make your birdbath as fresh as new by emptying the water, then covering it with bleach-soaked paper towels or newspaper. After letting the paper sit for 5–10 minutes, remove it and rinse the bath thoroughly. Then fill it with fresh water and watch the birds enjoy.

All-Natural Birdbath Saver There's a chemical in lavender that inhibits the growth of algae. Make a bundle of lavender flowers and daylily leaves for your birdbath to keep it crystal clear—and smelling wonderful! Change every few weeks.

See Also . . . For cleaning tips for inside your home, see the Cleaning Made Easy chapter!

chapter 5

All-Natural Pest Repellents

DIY Bug Sprays

Keeping Pests Out of Your Yard

Plant Savers

Keeping Pests Out of Your Home

DIY Bug Sprays

Natural Bug Spray If you're uncomfortable with all of the unpronounceable ingredients in commercial bug sprays, try making this natural version. Mix together ¼ cup apple cider vinegar, ¼ cup witch hazel, and around 20 drops of a combination of any the following essential oils: rosemary, citronella, tea tree, cedar, eucalyptus, or lemongrass. Transfer the mixture to a spray bottle, and shake before each use. Spray directly on exposed skin and the bugs will stay away!

Bug-Busting Lotion Bars You may have seen lotion bars in bath and beauty shops—they look like soaps, but you rub them on dry skin like lotion. Here's a great version that also doubles as a bug repellent. In a double boiler, stir together ½ cup coconut oil, 2 tablespoons each of dried rosemary and catnip (available at pet stores), 1 tablespoon dried thyme, and ½ teaspoon each of ground cloves and ground cinnamon. Once the coconut oil has melted, cover the mixture and allow it to cook for 15 to 20 minutes, until slightly darkened. (Periodically check the water levels in the bottom of the pan, adding more if needed). Strain the mixture and return it to the double boiler. Then add ¼ cup cocoa butter and ¼ cup plus 1 tablespoon beeswax. Stir until melted, and then remove from the heat. Add 5 drops each of lavender essential oil and lemon essential oil. Pour the mixture into silicone ice cube or candy molds. Allow the bars to set overnight until hard. To use, just rub a bar against exposed skin. Your skin will be moisturized, and bugs will find someone else to pester!

Who Knew? Classic Tip

If flies, bees, or other flying insects have invaded your home and you want to get them away from you fast, squirt a little hair spray into the air. They hate the stuff and will go elsewhere. It's not as good as a real bug spray, but it will do in a pinch!

Get Rid of Chiggers There may be nothing more disgusting in this world than chiggers. You can pick them up in the woods, and they will lay eggs in the folds of your skin, causing a poison ivy–like rash. If you think you've been exposed to chiggers, take a hot bath. The heat will cause the larvae to die, making your pain (and disgust!) short-lived.

Beat Bugs with Vicks Spending some time outdoors? Rub some Vicks VapoRub on your wrists and ankles to repel insects. They hate the smell and will leave you alone!

who knew? THE BIG QUESTION

Good-Bye, Mosquitoes

Mosquitoes love me! They downright attack me when I'm outside. How can I keep them away naturally?

—Stephanie Lynskey, via Facebook

Know What to Buy When shopping for a natural mosquito repellent, look for one that contains oil of lemon eucalyptus. It's extremely effective and provides long-lasting protection.

Mosquito Secret Mosquitoes are attracted to dark blue clothing. (It's true!) If you usually have trouble with mosquitoes, trying wearing light, pastel clothes when you're outdoors.

Peppermint Power Combine a few drops peppermint essential oil with 1 cup water in a spray bottle, shake well, and spray onto skin. Not only will the chemical compounds in peppermint help repel the blood-sucking beasts, but you'll also smell minty fresh!

Repel with Peels Another ingenious way to keep mosquitoes at bay? Rub exposed skin with orange or lemon peels. Mosquitoes hate the smell and will find someone else to attack.

Catnip Repellent Our friends swear by this mosquito remedy —as long as you don't have cats. Just rub fresh catnip leaves over exposed skin! It's easy to grow, so you can even plant some in your garden and pick the leaves for instant, all-natural mosquito protection.

No More Gnats Tiny little gnats are probably some of the most annoying bugs out there. When you see their telltale clouds, rub some baby oil on yourself to keep them away from you.

Remove Ticks with Ease Oh no, you've got a tick! If you're having trouble prying the little bugger off, apply a large glob of petroleum jelly to the area. Wait about 20 minutes, and you should be able to wipe him off with ease.

Fight Flies Are giant horseflies driving you crazy? Next time you go outside, rub mouthwash on your body and enjoy the serenity of a fly-free experience.

Keeping Pests Out of Your Yard

Let Nature Take Its Course Did you know that you can reduce the number of mosquitoes around your property just by attracting the right birds? Many birds—such as chickadees, orioles, finches, cardinals, and others—eat both seeds and insects. The trick is to give these birds what they're looking for, so fill feeders with sunflower and safflower seeds, or use suet feeders. The birds will stop by your place to eat, and then make a dent in the mosquito population while they're at it.

For a Bug-Free Fire Keep bugs from crashing your party by throwing some sage into the fire pit. They don't like the odor and will stay away. You can also add sage to your charcoal at a barbecue. It will keep the bugs away and give your food some earthy sage flavor.

Eliminate Bugs with Cinnamon Keep bugs out of your child's sandbox by spreading a cup or so of ground cinnamon into the sand. Ants, centipedes, and other pests will steer clear, so your child can play in peace.

Help for a Scorpion Problem Unfortunately, there aren't many natural remedies for getting rid of scorpions, one of the scariest-looking bugs ever! If you have a scorpion problem, start by clearing away piles of firewood or other debris from around the outside of your house, which will eliminate places where scorpions like to live. Scorpions also enjoy eating bugs like ants and roaches, so if you can eliminate those insects, you have a good chance of eliminating your scorpion problem too.

Have Your Way with Wasps To keep wasps far from your outdoor party, distract and trap them with this tip. In a small saucepan, heat 1 cup water and 1 cup sugar until the sugar is fully dissolved. Then pour a little of the mixture in paper cups, cover with foil, and secure with a rubber band. Punch a few holes in the foil of each cup. Set the cups in different locations around your yard, so that the wasps are drawn to them. They'll find their way into the cup, but will get trapped inside.

One Way In, No Way Out In summer, yellow jackets can be a big nuisance, not to mention a source of very painful stings. Lure them into a trap they won't be able to escape from, so you can enjoy the great outdoors in peace. Cut a small tab about an inch long in the side of an empty milk jug, and push the tab partially inside the container. Next, fill it with a few cups of fruit juice, and hang it on a tree branch. The yellow jackets will be attracted to the sweet fruit juice, will climb inside the container, and be unable to get out again.

Reusable Repellent Jar Here's a creative idea for keeping insects (particularly flies and mosquitoes) away from your next barbecue or outdoor party. You'll need an old tin or a Mason jar with a lid, as well as a clean cloth or rag. Saturate the cloth with a diluted essential oil like euca-

who knew? THE BIG QUESTION

Getting Rid of Ants

Is there any way to keep ants off of my deck? **—Kristen Cavallo O'Dell, via Facebook**

Raw Garlic Ant Repellent Obviously, it's hard not to feel like you're fighting a losing battle when you're trying to keep ants off your deck. But here's a trick you can try: Slice up some garlic cloves, and stick the slivers in between the cracks in the boards. The ants will stay clear of the garlic.

Our Vote: Vinegar One of the easiest ways to keep ants off your patio, picnic table, or other surfaces is with white vinegar. Put the vinegar in a spray bottle, and spray onto surfaces before your barbecue. It will keep the ants from smelling the food.

Adios Ants! Did you know ants won't cross charcoal? Take a piece of charcoal, crumble it up, and spread the pieces around the perimeter of your deck. The ants will avoid the area, leaving you to enjoy the food!

Extinguish Anthills If you find an ant nest outside, eliminate it by sprinkling cornmeal nearby. They'll eat it, but they can't digest it, and they'll begin to die out. Wait a couple of weeks and see if your ant problem improves.

lyptus, pennyroyal, peppermint, lavender, or lemongrass; place the cloth in the tin or jar and seal. To use, open the jar and place it on whatever table you'll be using outdoors. Its fragrance will repel insects. After every few uses, refresh the cloth with more diluted essential oil.

Who Knew? Classic Tip

Deer are beautiful, but they can be a huge nuisance in your garden. Keep them away from your precious plants with some slivers of a scented bar soap. Using a vegetable peeler, peel slivers of soap off into your garden. Deer will smell the soap and think humans are nearby, and will find someone else's garden to invade.

Fresh Herbs for Flies Flies don't like mint and basil, so if you want to keep the little pests away from your next barbecue, put a few bunches around the food. They'll look and smell great—to humans—and the flies will head elsewhere.

Deer Deterrent The deer in your neighborhood seem to think you planted a garden just for them! To ensure that you actually get to eat the fruits (and vegetables) of your labor, hang some dryer sheets around your garden. The smell will keep the deer away.

Out with Opossums If possums are a problem in your yard, mix together camphor oil with enough petroleum jelly to make a paste, and spread it around the base of trees. The smell should keep them away.

Who Knew? Classic Tip

Make sure squirrels, mice, and other critters don't chew through the rubber pipeline that connects your propane tank with your grill—reinforce the entire thing with duct tape. This is a good idea for anything else in your yard made out of rubber, as this is a favorite chew toy of rodents!

Peppermint for Pests Gophers hate the aroma of peppermint. Try planting mint near your home—chances are you will never see a gopher again! For a preexisting gopher problem, soak cotton balls in peppermint oil and then drop them down all the gopher holes you can find.

Good-bye to Moles Moles are pretty cute, until they're wreaking havoc on your yard. Use this all-natural solution to get rid of them: Just soak some old rags in olive oil, then stuff them in all the holes you can find. Moles hate the smell and will stay away.

Bird Fortress Nothing's more irritating than putting out a nice meal for the birds and watching a team of rodents skitter around the birdhouse with their cheeks popping out. Keep the squirrels away so the birds can eat. Cover the bird feeder pole or rope with petroleum jelly and they won't be able to scramble up (or down) into the feeder.

Who Knew? Classic Tip

If birds or squirrels are nibbling at your fruit trees, try hanging long strips of aluminum foil from the branches. They'll be attracted to its shiny surface, but once they bite it, they'll scamper away.

So Long, Skunks Mothballs aren't just for moths! Sprinkle them around your yard, and they'll keep skunks away. Just be careful, as they're harmful to your pet should he decide to eat them!

Easy Snake Deterrent If you spot a garden snake and wish it would go elsewhere, it can be as easy as reaching for the hose. Spray the snake until he slithers away, hopefully before you get the creeps.

Befuddle Birds Birds (and their droppings) driving you crazy on your deck? Keep them away with baking or baby powder. Sprinkle it where they like to land, and they'll find somewhere else to go. They hate the feeling of it under their feet!

Anti-Snake Solution If snakes seem to always find their way into your yard, keep them away with ammonia. Soak rags in ammonia and place them in unsealed plastic bags. Leave the plastic bags where you usually see the snakes, and you'll never see them again! Snakes hate the smell of ammonia and won't come near it.

Plant Savers

Orange Peels for Slugs and Snails To keep slugs and snails from destroying your garden, place some orange peels on the soil. The creepy crawlers are attracted by the peels and will begin to feed on them out in the open. You can collect and remove them from the garden.

Scram, Caterpillars! Get rid of caterpillars the same way you'd get rid of vampires: with garlic. Mix 1 cup water with 1 tablespoon garlic powder or one minced clove of garlic. Then add a squirt of dishwashing liquid, which will help the concoction stick to leaves and stems. Pour into a spray bottle and spray on plants once every few days to keep caterpillars away.

Who Knew? Classic Tip

Need to get rid of snails or slugs in your garden? Find the cheapest beer you can, then pour it into several shallow containers (shoeboxes lined with aluminum foil work well). Dig a few shallow holes in your garden and place the containers inside so that they are at ground level. Leave overnight, and the next morning, you'll find dozens of dead (or drunk) snails and slugs inside. These critters are attracted to beer (who isn't?), but it has a diuretic effect on them, causing them to lose vital liquids and die.

Houseplant Insect Spray Say good-bye to insects in your plants with this formula, which is especially great for meal bugs. Just pour 2 to 3 tablespoons of dry laundry soap and 1 quart of warm water into a spray container and shake well. Spray the solution onto plants immediately;

this solution cannot be stored and must be made fresh for each use.

Shell Game To keep slugs and snails away from your plants, sprinkle some crushed eggshells around the base. This is also a great way of adding needed calcium to the soil. Whenever you use an egg in a recipe, you can rinse out the shell, crush it, and store it in a container for this purpose!

Who Knew? Classic Tip

Sometimes, getting rid of insects is as easy as making it hard for them to get where they're going. Smear petroleum jelly around the base of plant stems, and ants and other crawling insects will slide right off, protecting your plants.

Mighty Mite Treatment Red spider mites can be extremely destructive to plants, damaging leaves and slowing growth. In extreme cases, they can even kill a plant. To eliminate them, spray your plants every week with a mild soap spray. Once the problem is under control, reduce the treatments to once a month.

Save a Plant from Spider Mites Have you noticed tiny, fragile webs on your houseplants? You probably have spider mites living there. To get rid of them, gently wipe some buttermilk on the leaves and stems. They should disappear, leaving your plants healthy and green again.

Whitefly Remover Whiteflies are tiny insects similar to aphids that can destroy plants. They chew on plants and leave a sticky substance that can also kill them. To kill whiteflies before they kill your plants, spray the plants with this mixture: 2 cups water, ¾ cup rubbing alcohol, and a generous squirt of dishwashing liquid. Repeat after it rains to keep whiteflies away for good.

Potato Water Prescription Making sweet potatoes for dinner? Save the water you boil them in and put it into a spray bottle. Spray the liquid wherever you see ants or aphids on your houseplants, and they'll become a thing of the past.

Cure for Cutworms If you've come outside to find your plants' stems cut as if by a tiny axe, you have a cutworm problem. But you can fix it with an item you probably usually recycle: a cardboard paper towel or toilet paper tube. If you're using a paper towel tube, cut it in half first. Then place it over your plant so that in encircles the stem. Bury it so that an inch of the tube is underground, and it will protect your precious plants.

No More Aphids Save your plants from aphids with this simple formula: Boil 1 pint of water and add 1 lemon's worth of zest. Let steep overnight. In the morning, strain the rind if desired. Pour liquid into a spray bottle and spray it on your plants. Soon, aphids will be a thing of the past.

Who Knew? Classic Tip

Keep your rosebush the pride of your garden by getting rid of those icky Japanese beetles. Pour a bowl of self-rising flour and go outside, sprinkling it over the whole bush like it's some kind of magic potion (which, in this case, it is).

Pet-Proof the Garden Instead of throwing out orange, lemon, and lime peels, chop them up for use in your garden! If you sprinkle citrus rinds directly on the soil, you'll keep cats, dogs, and other neighborhood animals away from your plants.

A "Fresh" Way to Fight Squirrels Squirrels can be one of the trickiest garden pests to deal with. They chomp on flower bulbs and other leaves, dig up your favorite plants, and otherwise wreak havoc. Protect your garden by grating some Irish Spring soap around your plants. Squirrels can't stand the smell of it and will stay away.

Molasses for Moths and Grubs Moths and grubs can be a big problem with garden plants like corn, broccoli, cauliflower, cabbage, and other crops. To keep them from munching on your plants, make a molasses spray. In a spray bottle combine 4 cups water, 1 tablespoon molasses, and 1 teaspoon dishwashing detergent. Spray this mixture all over the leaves of your plants weekly.

Fake It with a Snake Keep birds away from your garden by putting a rubber snake in it. As they fly overhead, they'll see the fake serpent and won't land near it. (Just make sure you tell family members it's there, or you could give your kids quite a shock when you send them out to pick string beans!)

Rhubarb-Leaf Garden Spray Rhubarb leaves are poisonous and can't be eaten; however, you can use them to help fight garden pests like whiteflies and caterpillars.

In a bucket, crush some rhubarb leaves, and pour boiling water over them to cover. Allow the mixture to steep for a few days, and strain into a spray bottle. Add a squirt of dishwashing soap and a bit of water to dilute it. Spray on the leaves of your plants every seven to 10 days.

Who Knew? Classic Tip

If you want to keep bugs off your plants, try spraying their leaves with a solution of 10 parts weak tea and one part ammonia. Try it first on a few leaves to test for damage, and make sure pets and children don't try to eat or lick the leaves (hey, they've done weirder things!).

Rabbit-Repelling Plants If rabbits eat your garden year after year, try planting plants that repel them. These include amaryllis, bleeding hearts, daylilies, English ivy, ferns, forget-me-nots, foxglove, impatiens, and pachysandra. Rabbits also hate certain trees, such as cedar, magnolia, maple, oak, pine, and spruce.

Eradicate Raccoons Raccoons keep getting into your trash, and so far your only strategy is running outside to yell at them every night. Save your screaming and purchase some inexpensive Epsom salts from a drugstore.

Sprinkle them on and around your garbage cans and raccoons will stay away, but your pets will be safe!

A News Solution Lure earwigs away from your plants by placing flowerpots filled with crumpled-up newspaper in your garden. The earwigs will hide in the newspaper, and in the morning, you can shake them out into a bucket of hot water, or simply throw the paper away.

Keeping Pests Out of Your Home

Put an End to Pantry Moths When you buy dry goods, you could unknowingly be bringing pantry moth eggs home with you. To avoid an infestation, stick these items in the freezer for a week before storing them. You'll kill any eggs that might have hitched a ride home with you, and your pantry will stay a pest-free zone.

Swap Mothballs for Lavender Oil When you store your off-season wardrobe, skip the toxic mothballs and choose lavender oil instead. Add several drops of lavender oil to cotton balls, and tie them up in a sachet (you can use cheesecloth or even an old nylon). You'll repel any pests who might want to munch on your items, and when you take your clothes out again, they'll have a lovely lavender smell.

Banish Moths with Basil There's nothing quite like the sweet smell of basil, right? Not for moths! They hate the smell. Keep some around the house and moths will be a thing of the past.

Who Knew? Classic Tip

Placing your woolen clothes in a well-sealed bag isn't always enough to keep moths away, as any eggs laid in them beforehand will hatch—and the new moths will have a field day. To make sure all the eggs die before you put your clothes in storage, place the airtight bag of clothes in the freezer for 24 hours.

Repel Ants with Cucumber Spring finally arrived, and so did the ants! To get rid of them, find the spots where they're entering your home, and place some cucumber peels there. Ants find cucumber repellent and will stay away.

who knew? THE BIG QUESTION

Keeping Spiders Away

I hate spiders!! Is there any way to keep them out of my house?

—LaTrelle Walker, via Facebook

Nuts for Spiders Spiders can actually be beneficial to have around, since they'll kill other household bugs for you. But if you can't handle their creepiness, try putting out whole walnuts in their shell in corners, on windowsills, or wherever you tend to see the spiders. Walnut shells contain a chemical toxic to spiders, and they'll stay away.

Cedar Does It Who knew spiders don't like cedar? If you have a spider problem in your home, just put some cedar chips into a few pairs of old pantyhose and hang them around your house. The spiders will be gone in no time.

Hedge Your Bets If you live in a part of the country where hedge apples grow, you can use the fruits to repel spiders. Just place a few wherever you tend to see spiders hang out in your home.

A Spidey-Free Zone Spiders hate citrus, so try this nontoxic repellent. In a spray bottle, mix together 2 cups water with 1½ teaspoons citrus essential oil (such as orange, lemon, or lime). Spray wherever you see spiders or their webs, and the citrus will send them packing!

Moth Trap Trap moths by mixing one part molasses with two parts white vinegar and placing the mixture in a bright yellow container. The moths will be attracted to the color and the smell, then drown inside.

Spicy Ant Barricade The arrival of spring brings warm temperatures, breezy open windows, backyard dining, and—unfortunately—an influx of ants. To keep those wily bugs from sneaking into your home, ditch the store-bought chemicals and reach for the spice rack instead! Mix red pepper flakes and sage, then sprinkle around the pantry and along window sills and doorways to keep ants from marching in.

Who Knew? Classic Tip

Swatting at bees is unnecessary (and never leads to anything good). Just turn out the light and open a window. The light from outside will attract them even more than your nice, juicy arm.

A Better Home for Ladybugs If you've noticed that ladybugs find your home an attractive place to hang out in the winter, you can use this simple strategy to reduce their numbers without actually killing them. (After all, they actually don't do any damage to your home.) Fill a shoebox with some fruit scraps like apple pieces, and place it where you see the bugs. The fruit will attract the bugs, and you can then move them out into the garage where they should hibernate until spring.

Who Knew? Classic Tip

If you can figure out where ants are entering your house, you can keep them out. Simply sprinkle salt, cinnamon, chalk dust, or ashes on the their path of entry, and they'll turn around and go elsewhere.

Never Buy Flypaper Again To get rid of crickets or other critters, place packaging tape sticky-side-up along the wall in your basement or wherever else you find them. This inexpensive flypaper will snag them so you can stomp them out and throw them away.

Getting Rid of Bedbugs Bedbugs usually require a professional exterminator, but if you have a mild infestation, you might be able to tackle them on your own. You'll need a powerful vacuum—the plug-in canister kind work well, but something battery-operated or upright usually won't do the trick. Vacuum all carpet, baseboards, switch plates, wallpaper creases, appliances, and any cracks you can find. Wash the vacuum canister with hot water to kill any eggs that may be there. Next, hit up these same areas with a substance called diatomaceous earth, which you can find in pet stores or gardening stores. It dehydrates the bed bugs and thereby kills them, so sprinkle it or smear it everywhere you think the bedbugs may be living, including on the floor near your bed, all over your bed frame, and in any cracks in the wall near your bed.

Bedbug-Proof Your Mattress To get rid of bedbugs, you'll have to make sure that they'll never again visit that soft, comfy home that gives them their name: your bed. To get bedbugs our of your bed, first strip it of all bedding and wash and dry it on the highest heat setting available. Then thoroughly vacuum your mattress and box spring, focusing carefully on every crease and crevice. This means taking the fabric sheeting off of the box spring and getting inside of it. When done, seal the mattress and box spring inside bedbug-proof plastic bags made for mattresses and box springs. It's recommended that you leave the bags on for an entire year, simply putting the sheets and any mattress pads right on top of the bags.

Clean Up the Stink If you have a big stinkbug problem in your home, it's time to spray down your house! To stop them from entering your home, mix together 1 quart hot water with 3/4 cup dishwashing liquid. Spray the outside of your house with this mixture, focusing on cracks, crevices, windows, and doors.

Keep Stinkbugs Out Another way to keep pesky stinkbugs out of your house is by starting with your window screens. Vigorously wipe down the outside of screens with fabric softener sheets, and it will help repel the critters. The fabric softener sticks to the screen, and the stinkbugs hate the smell and the feel.

Who Knew? Classic Tip

If you prefer not to use chemicals to get rid of flies, and you're not the most accurate fly swatter, invest in a strong fan. Scientists say that flies' wings are unable to operate in a breeze above nine mph, so open the windows, turn the fan to full power, and they'll soon buzz off.

Better Bean Storage If you've ever had weevils infest your dry goods, you'll take us up on this tip. If you're storing dry beans in your pantry, toss a dried hot pepper into the container. It will deter weevils.

Natural Roach Killer Nothing is more revolting than roaches, except perhaps the chemicals we use to kill them. Try using this natural pesticide: Make a mixture of equal parts cornstarch and plaster of Paris, and sprinkle it in the cracks where roaches appear. If you're lucky, they'll be a thing of the past.

Who Knew? Classic Tip

Another great method for eliminating cockroaches is to fill a large bowl with cheap wine, then place it under the sink or wherever you see the revolting little bugs. The pests drink the wine, get drunk, and drown.

Good-Bye, Mealworms Never worry about mealworms getting into your pasta, rice, or flour again! Just spread bay leaves around your cabinets. Mealworms hate the smell, and will stay away.

Mice Mind Vinegar Make your home a less attractive place for mice by placing cotton balls soaked with white vinegar wherever you see the little critters: under cabinets, in closets, in corners, and so on. Mice find the smell of vinegar unappealing and will avoid it. Be sure to change the cotton balls frequently so that the vinegar smell remains fresh.

Get a Leg Up on Centipedes Borax works for repelling centipedes and millipedes. Sprinkle around areas where you've spotted them making a run for it. (Also works for the less offensive crickets.) Borax is an inexpensive cleaner than can be found at larger supermarkets, home stores, and discount retailers. Unfortunately, it isn't pet- or kid-safe, so sprinkle wisely.

Who Knew? Classic Tip

Silverfish are disgusting, down to each and every one of their legs. An effective, natural way to repel them is with whole cloves. Just sprinkle a few in drawers and other areas where you see them.

Fat Chance Here's a tip for rodent control that is quite effective, but might not be for the faint of heart! If you're looking to kill mice, put out a bowl of instant mashed potato flakes and a bowl of water. The rodents will eat the dry potato flakes, and when they drink the water, their stomachs will expand so much they'll die.

Get Out and Stay Out If you have a rat problem, you know how tenacious the little buggers are. We haven't had much luck with natural remedies that get rid of other rodents—such as leaving bay leaves or mint around. Rats will eat anything! The most effective way to solve a rat infestation is to seal closed every way in which they're entering your house. To help you figure it out, sprinkle baby powder on your floor before going to sleep. In the morning, you'll find paw prints where they're getting in. Seal all holes with caulk, or stuff steel wool inside. Rats will no longer be able to get into your home.

Who Knew? Classic Tip

If you're squeamish about having to pick up the remains of a rodent you've set a trap for, place the baited trap inside a brown paper lunch bag. Rodents like exploring small spaces, and once the trap has done its trick, you can scoop it right up and throw it away.

How to Bait a Rat Trap If you're baiting a rat trap, there are a few things you should know. First, make sure to wear latex gloves while baiting the trap. Rats have a highly developed sense of smell, and if they smell the scent of humans on the trap, they'll stay away. The best foods to use in a rat trap are their favorite treats: bread, bananas, soft cheese like Cheddar, and raw bacon. Place near any water sources or sites where you've found rat droppings.

Rodent Remover at the Ready It won't surprise you if you've ever smelled them, but mothballs repel rodents, too. To use them to get rid of mice or rats around your home, place five of them in a Ziploc bag and smash until they're a powder. Then put in a spray bottle along with a squirt of dishwashing liquid and fill with water. Spray around baseboards and anywhere you see pests, but keep away from kids and pets.

Pests Hate Mint If you have a mouse or rat in your house, head to the nearest health store and pick up some peppermint essential oil. Add about a dozen drops to a spray bottle filled with water, and shake. Then spray anywhere you've seen or heard the critters. They hate the smell of mint and will find somewhere else to hang out.

See Also . . . For tips on getting rid of fleas, see the Smart Pet Tricks chapter.

chapter 6

Cleaning Made Easy

Kitchen Cleaning Tricks

Dishes and Dining

Easy Bathroom Cleaning

Sweeping and Vacuuming

Surprising Furniture Cleaners

Quick Cleans for Household Objects

Kitchen Cleaning Tricks

Spring Cleaning for Kitchen Cabinets Your wooden kitchen cabinets may look clean, but over time, they can develop a sticky film. To eliminate it, mix one part vegetable oil with two parts baking soda, and rub on the cabinets. Remove the paste with a damp cloth, and then dry with a clean rag. You'll be surprised at how much brighter they look!

Germ-Killing Kitchen Cleaner Tea tree oil is a little-known cleaning heavyweight—a natural nontoxic antiseptic, it will kill any lingering germs, bacteria, and fungi on linoleum countertops and floors. We add a few drops of tea tree oil to hydrogen peroxide when attacking linoleum kitchen floors.

Marble Maintenance Marble countertops add a touch of elegance to a home, but unfortunately, they can't be cleaned with most commercial products. We recommend the old-fashioned route. First, fill a small basin or your sink with warm water, and add a drop or two of dishwashing liquid. With a sponge, use the soapy water to wipe down the countertop, then rinse and dry the area. If you notice a stain, add a few drops of bleach to baking soda until you've made a paste, cover the stain with it, and leave overnight. The next day, wet the area and remove the paste, and be sure to rinse the area thoroughly.

Get Rid of Stone Stains To remove stains on stone countertops, make a mixture of warm water with a few drops of both hydrogen peroxide and ammonia. Rub it into the stain, wait a few minutes, then rinse with warm water. To eliminate small scratches, you can buff with superfine steel wool.

Who Knew? Classic Tip

When you're done with an afternoon of baking, here's an easy way to clean the stuck-on dough from your counter: Just sprinkle your messy countertop with salt, and you'll be able to use a damp sponge to easily wipe away the doughy, floury mess you've left behind.

Streaky Clean Stainless steel appliances are incredibly popular these days, but they can be tricky to keep clean. To get rid of those unsightly streaks and fingerprints, put a little bit of oil on a dry dishcloth, and rub down the appliance. Then buff with a dry paper towel for a glossy finish.

(Not So) Permanent Marker To remove a marker stain (even from permanent marker) from a countertop, use an orange peel. First, rub the outside with your fingers to bring the orange oil to the surface, then rub the peel directly on the marker stain. You may need to use a little elbow grease, but it will come out!

Who Knew? Classic Tip

When cleaning your refrigerator, don't use chemicals that can linger on your food and create nasty odors. After emptying the fridge, simply dissolve a cup of salt in a gallon of hot water and wipe away. Squeeze in the juice of a lemon for a nice scent.

Stainless Steel Scratch Healer If you find a scratch on one of your stainless steel appliances, buff it out with superfine steel wool, which you should be able to find at a hardware store. Then polish any rough spots with a wax-based aerosol spray (search for it online), which is a cleaner made just for stainless steel.

Make Black Appliances Gleam Vinegar can help remove streaks on black appliances. After cleaning them with warm, sudsy water and a sponge, rub them with a rag dampened with straight white vinegar. The vinegar will remove soap residue and make your appliances shine.

A Clean Ice Dispenser It's so convenient to have a refrigerator with built-in ice and water dispensers, but you may have noticed how gross the dispenser tray can look after a while. That whitish, mineral buildup seems impossible to wash off with soapy water, but vinegar will do the trick. Soak the tray in straight vinegar for a few minutes, then scrub the stains with an old toothbrush. Rinse with warm water, and your dispenser will look like new again!

Eliminate Odors with Oatmeal Out of baking soda and need to freshen up the fridge? Try oatmeal! An open container of dry oats in the fridge will neutralize odors just as well as baking soda does.

Repurpose Plastic Placemats For easy-to-clean fruit and vegetable drawers, line them with old plastic placemats you've cut to size. That way, when you need to clean the drawers (for example, when you've found a fuzzy orange or oozing pepper!), you can just remove the placements and wipe them down. It's much easier than trying to clean each groove at the bottom of the drawer.

Under-the-Fridge Duster Crumbs and dirt get everywhere in our kitchen—but the worst of all are those sneaky rascals that scatter beneath the fridge and oven. To nab that hard-to-reach dirt, we use a snowbrush that's intended for the car. The narrow brush is a perfect fit for the tight space, and its long handle reaches way back to the wall.

Immaculate Magnets Clean refrigerator magnets in seconds with help from some old pantyhose. Cut the foot off an old pair and place the magnets inside, then tie the pantyhose shut. Place in the utensil compartment of your dishwasher and the nylon will protect your magnets while still allowing the warm suds through.

Microwave Cleaning Trick To clean your microwave oven, soak several paper towels in water, then stick them in the microwave and heat on high for three minutes. (Keep an eye on them to make sure they don't dry out.) The steam will help release the built-up dirt. Once the towels cool, you can use them to easily wipe down the interior.

De-Gunk the Toaster Oven With all of its small parts, the toaster oven can be a tricky appliance to keep clean. Make the process easier with this tip: Fill a small, oven-safe baking dish with water and place it inside the toaster oven. Heat the oven to 350°F, and leave for 10 to 15 minutes. The water will convert to steam, helping to soften the crumbs and burnt-on foods so that you can wipe the oven down. Just be sure to unplug it and let it cool down before you start cleaning!

Stove Saver Here's a tip to impress even your friend who has a superhuman level of household know-how: Use tea to keep gunk from sticking to your stove. Brew a pot of tea that is four times normal strength, then wipe it on your stove. The tannins in the tea will make it hard for grease and food to stick, making cleaning quick and easy.

Who Knew? Classic Tip

Here's the easiest way we've found to clean a countertop grill: Unplug it, then put a wet paper towel inside and close the lid for 10 minutes. The grease will be loosened up and easy to clean off.

For a Clean Coffee Grinder If you grind your own coffee beans, you know what a difference the fresh flavor makes in your morning cup of java. To maintain that great taste, give your grinder a periodic cleaning to eliminate stale flavors. Once a week, put a few tablespoons of sugar into the grinder, and let it run for one to two minutes. Dump the sugar out and wipe the insides clean.

Remove Melted Plastic We've all done it: You place a loaf of bread on top of a still-hot toaster oven, and a piece of the plastic bag melts to the metal. Luckily, there's an easy way to remove it: Rub a bit of Vaseline on the stuck plastic, and then turn on the toaster so that it heats up. Then rub the area with a paper towel until the plastic comes off.

Unclog Gas Burners Thanks to a spill, the burners on your gas range are clogged with last night's dinner. Open up the holes with one of your child's pipe cleaners. They're narrow enough to get into that small space. And isn't it satisfying to actually clean something with a pipe cleaner?

Clean Oil with Oil Clean oily splatters on your stove or range hood with—oil! Though it seems a bit counterintuitive, this trick works like a dream. Place some mineral oil on a paper towel and rub away stove splatters (if you don't have mineral oil, olive oil will also work). The oil will pick up the dirt and leave behind a protective film, so that it's easier to clean next time. If you are using oil

who knew? THE BIG QUESTION

Easy Oven Cleaning

Oven cleaning is definitely my most-dreaded kitchen chore. Can you help?

—Samantha Gersten, via WhoKnewTips.com

Vinegar Can Help Commercial oven cleaners are very effective, but the fumes could knock down an elephant! To help reduce fumes after you've used a powerful oven cleaner, wipe down the inside of the oven with white vinegar. It will remove any remaining residue and help to neutralize the cleaner.

The Black Bag Treatment Make your oven racks easier to clean by adding a bit of oven cleaner to them, placing them in a black plastic trash bag, and setting them outside in the sun. (You don't have to coat the racks, because the fumes caught in the bag will do most of the work.) After a few hours, they'll be ready to spray off with a hose.

Non-Oven Cleaner Method A simple way to clean your oven without using an oven cleaner is to place an oven-safe pot or bowl filled with water inside. Heat on 450° for 20 minutes, and the steam will loosen the dirt and grease. Once your oven is cool, wipe off the condensation and the grease will come with it. When you're done, make a paste of water and baking soda and smear it on any enamel. The paste will dry into a protective layer that will absorb grease as you cook.

to clean a glass stovetop, however, be sure to wash it off afterward, so that the oil doesn't burn when you next turn on the stove.

Orange Oven A self-cleaning oven can leave an odor after it's done its work. Eliminate the lingering smell by turning down the oven to 350° after the cleaning cycle, then placing a baking sheet lined with orange peels on the middle rack. Cook the peels for a half an hour, and not only will the oven smell fresh, but your whole kitchen will too!

Deep-Clean the Dishwasher If you're anything like us, your dishwasher gets a lot of action. So don't forget that it needs a bit of maintenance too. Give this super-powered cleaning machine its own well-deserved day at the spa: Pour 1 cup white vinegar into an open dishwasher-safe container (any cup will do). Place it in the top rack of the machine and start the hot cycle. For round two, pour baking soda along the bottom of the dishwasher and start a short wash cycle. The double-duty wash will leave it fresh, shiny, and ready for action!

Superpower Your Dishwasher Strong food odors like fish and onion can linger on dishware and utensils even after a good machine-wash. Give those stinky items an extra dose of cleaning power by mixing a teaspoon of baking soda with your usual detergent. Then just use as you normally would for super-clean dishes!

Remove Sink Spots Polish a stainless-steel sink and kill germs by rubbing it down with rubbing alcohol. The alcohol is great at removing water spots.

Who Knew? Classic Tip

Instead of throwing away baking soda away when it's finished its 30-day stint in your fridge, dump it down the garbage disposal with running water. It will keep your disposal fresh too!

Cleaner Chrome Keep your chrome fixtures looking cleaner longer by polishing them with car wax. The wax will create a barrier against water spots, soap scum, and other stains, so that cleaning will be easier next time. Just rub the wax onto your fixtures as if they were cars!

A Lemony-Fresh Kitchen To give your kitchen a lemon-fresh scent, you don't need to buy expensive air fresheners. Just use a real lemon! Poke a few holes in it with a toothpick or skewer, then place it directly on the rack in a 300° oven for 15 minutes. Leave the oven door slightly ajar so that the wonderful aroma can permeate the whole room. Alternatively, you can slice a lemon and boil it in some water on the stovetop for 10 to 15 minutes as well.

Soothing Spicy Scents To easily deodorize your kitchen, put a cinnamon stick and other favorite spices (such as cloves or ginger) in a mug of water, and microwave it for two minutes. Remove the mug and set it on the counter so that the aroma can fill the kitchen. This trick is great for winter, when the scent of the spices will create a warm, cozy atmosphere.

Dishes and Dining

Make Your Dish Soap More Powerful Did you know that the acetic acid in vinegar dramatically increases the cleaning power of soap? Boost your dishwashing liquid's effectiveness by adding a couple teaspoons of white vinegar to the bottle (agitate gently to combine). You'll need less to get your dishes clean, saving you money!

Spectacularly Sparkling Dishes If your usual detergent leaves your dishware looking "blah" rather than bright, try this DIY solution instead—it'll make your glasses gleam and save you the cash you'd normally spend on brand-name soaps. Combine 1 cup borax, 1 cup baking soda, ¼ cup kosher salt, and ¼ cup citric acid. Use only 1 to 2 tablespoons of this solution plus 3 drops of liquid dish soap per load. Before you close the washer, toss ½ cup white vinegar onto the floor of the machine. Start the wash, and in no time, your dishes and glasses will be shinier than ever!

Magic for Mugs Get rid of really tough stains in your mugs by filling them with boiling water and adding a denture tablet. Let it sit overnight, and the stain should disappear.

Who Knew? Classic Tip

Who knew salt was the best way to remove lipstick from a glass? Rub a little over the stain to remove an imprint on the side of the glass, then wash as usual. Sticking lipstick-marked glasses in the dishwasher hardly ever works, because lipstick is made to resist water.

Peel Sessions The next time you're peeling apples, don't toss the peels—they can be used to bring the shine back to aluminum pots and pans! Just fill the pots with water and a few apple peels. Bring to a boil for several minutes, then let the water cool in the pot before discarding. The peels will restore shine to the aluminum.

Who Knew? Classic Tip

What if your nonstick pan starts sticking? For the most part, coated pots and pans are easy to keep clean, but they do stain, and over time grease and oil may build up. This will adversely affect the efficiency of the nonstick surface, so it's important to clean and re-season any stained areas. To do so, simply mix 1 cup water, 2 tablespoons baking soda, and ½ cup white vinegar in the pot, set on the stove, and boil for 10 minutes. Wash the pot as usual, then rub vegetable oil on the surface of the plastic coating to re-season it.

Cola Cleaner To remove caked-on food from a pan, it's cola to the rescue! Pour a can of cola into the empty skillet. Bring it to a boil, and the stains should scrape off more easily.

Skillet Saver The teriyaki chicken you made for dinner was delicious, but the sweet sauce left terrible black burns on the bottom of your frying pan. To clean it (or any other burnt-on food), first sprinkle the pan with ¼ to ½ cup baking soda, and fill the pan halfway with water. Bring the water to a boil, and the burned pieces should start to release. As the water boils, you can use a spatula to help the process along. When most of the pieces are removed, turn off the heat, dump the water, and wash as usual.

Absorb Fish Odors To neutralize fish odors on a cutting board, wash the board, then scrub it with mustard powder. Allow the powder to penetrate for a few minutes, then rinse with warm water. The smell will be gone!

Who Knew? Classic Tip

Steel wool or copper scrubbers are a must-have when cleaning heavy-duty pots, but they rust so easily! Solve this problem forever by placing the scrubber in a Ziploc bag in the freezer between each use. The cold air will freeze the water, making it unable to cause rust. When you need it again, just hold under warm water!

The Easy Way to Clean a Cheese Grater We love freshly grated cheese. It tastes so much fresher than the pre-grated packages you buy at the supermarket. But one of our least favorite cleaning tasks has to be washing the dirty grater. To make the process easier, we grate a piece of raw potato; it does the most difficult part of the cleaning for you!

So Long, Mashed Potato Mess Everybody loves silky-smooth mashed potatoes, but it's not always so much fun to clean up the potato masher or ricer afterward. The best strategy is to soak the masher in warm soapy water immediately after using it. When you get around to washing it, you'll have a much easier task.

Mucky Basting Brush? You've washed and washed your basting brush, and yet it still seems sticky. Soak it in a cup of straight vinegar for a few hours to help dissolve the greasy buildup, then wash as usual. It will be as good as new!

Spin the Bottle We like to know how to do everything the "right" way, and were happy to add this bottle-cleaning know-how to our list! To speed up the process of rinsing the suds out of a narrow-necked bottle or other slim jar, turn the bottle upside down and shake it in a circular motion. The whirlpool effect created will force the water to rush out more quickly and easily.

Wine Decanter Easy Clean Wine decanters are notoriously difficult to clean. Once you've finally got all of the suds out a of decanter, how do you dry it? There's no way your hand will fit down that narrow neck! Instead, roll up a paper towel, stick it down the neck of the decanter, and set aside for a few hours. The paper towel will absorb excess moisture so that the glass isn't stained with water spots.

Who Knew? Classic Tip

To remove odors from dishes, bottles, or plastic containers, add a teaspoon of mustard to hot water and let the item soak in it for five minutes, then wash as usual.

Tending to Teapots Whenever you boil hard water in a teapot, mineral deposits stick around in the pot and will eventually form a white chalky film that can clog it, inhibit its ability to heat up, and even affect the taste of your tea. To prevent hard water buildup, try this old-world (yet effective!) trick: Place a glass marble inside the kettle and boil water as usual—the marble will attract the mineral residue. Check on the marble every few weeks. When it seems loaded with buildup, simply swap the old marble for a new one.

A Tip to Keep on File With use, plastic kitchen utensils like spoons and spatulas can develop rough edges. To keep them looking their best, file the rough spots away with a clean emery board. They'll look like new!

Thermos Odor Eater You may have noticed that if you store a thermos or refillable water bottle in the cabinet for a long time, it starts to get a stale smell. Add a teaspoon of sugar before you put it away, and close the lid tightly. The sugar will stop those odors from forming; just rinse it before you use it again.

Who Knew? Classic Tip

Impossible-to-remove stains on your china? There may be hope yet. Apply a bit of nail polish remover to the spots with a soft cloth, then wash as usual. The spots should quickly fade.

Cleaner Candlesticks If you like to use candles at your holiday gatherings, you know what a pain it can be to clean the candle holders. Next time, try rubbing a little bit of petroleum jelly inside each holder. When the candle burns down, you'll be able to remove the remaining wax with ease, making holiday cleanup much faster.

Appealing Silver There's no need to buy silver polish full of toxic chemicals! A banana peel will do the job just as well. Wipe the inside of the peel on your candlesticks, silverware, or whatever else needs polishing. Then wipe off with a dry cloth for a shiny finish.

Easy Bathroom Cleaning

Spray Soap Scum Away! Ever wonder what makes that sticky sludge on your shower walls and tiles so darn hard to clean? It's a combination of mildew, soap residue, mineral deposits, hard water, and oils from your skin—and it's one of our most challenging household foes. To conquer the scum, we've started using cooking spray or vegetable oil as part of our cleaning regimen: The oils help break up the slimy coating of soap scum. Spray the oil all over the grimy areas, let sit 5 minutes, then wash off with soap and water and dry. Just make sure not to get it on the floor or tub, as it can be very slippery!

Fight Shower Scum with Lemon Power! A lemon is one mighty all-purpose cleaning tool—its antibacterial, antifungal, and antiviral properties along with its mild acids make it one of the best natural disinfectants around.

And yeah, it smells nice too! To attack that stubborn scum in the shower, we slice one lemon in half and dip it in a bowl of kosher salt, which adds an abrasive scrub to the already-powerful juices. Scrub the glass shower door and leave for a few minutes while the lemon gets to work. Rinse off with water, and say good-bye to scum!

Rubber Ducky, You're the (Moldy) One It's gross, but true: Your child's floating bath toys (the kinds with a hole in the bottom) are likely filled with allergy-causing mold. Even if you squeeze out the toys after every bath, some moisture remains and can cause mold buildup. To avoid this problem in the first place, seal the hole of a brand-new toy with hot glue. That way, water will never be able to penetrate it in the first place. To clean older toys, soak them in a solution of 1 cup bleach mixed with 1 gallon warm water for an hour or two to release the mold. Then scrub them, rinse, and allow them to dry completely before sealing.

Say Good-Bye to White Sink Stains If you have stubborn stains in a white sink and feel like you've tried everything to remove them, it's time to bring in the big guns: bleach. Line the bottom of the sink with paper towels and then soak them with bleach (just make sure that bleach is safe for the surface you're treating and that you're in a

who knew? THE BIG QUESTION

Cleaning Grout

No matter how hard I try, I can't seem to get the grout between the tiles of my shower clean! Help! **—Melissa Freeman, via Facebook**

Grout-Cleaning Miracle That immovable black line of mold on your grout can spoil an otherwise spotless space! That's why we love this clever tip, which uses a bleach pen that's intended for laundry stains. Simply trace over your grout lines with the pen and leave for 20 to 30 minutes. Wipe clean with a dampened towel, and voilà—your bathroom will be instantly brighter!

Around the Tub If you have mold buildup around the edge of your tub where it meets the wall, here's a way to get rid of it for good. You'll need bleach, a bucket, and a package of those cotton coils used for perms (you can find them at a beauty-supply store). Put the bucket in the shower, then add some bleach and soak the coils in it. Once they're saturated, take them out and line the edges of your tub with them. Allow the bleach to work on the stains overnight, then remove the coil, and rinse with water. If any stains remain, they should come right off with a scrub brush.

Keep It Clean Grab an old white candle or white crayon for the bathroom. Rubbing the wax onto your bathroom grout will help protect it from growing mold, mildew, and other stains in the future!

well-ventilated area), and wait 30 minutes. Rinse and let dry and the stains should finally be gone!

For a No-Scum Shower Curtain Show soap scum and mildew who's boss by adding hydrogen peroxide to your shower-curtain cleaning regimen. Stick the curtain and a bath towel into your washing machine, pour in regular detergent, and start the wash. Add 1 cup peroxide during the rinse cycle.

Who Knew? Classic Tip

If you have a pair of pinking shears (scissors with a zigzagging edge used in sewing), put them to good use in the bathroom. Use them to cut the bottom of your shower curtain liner: The uneven hem allows water to more easily slide off, making bottom-of-the-curtain mildew a thing of the past.

Stop Dirt in Its Tracks If you've ever wondered about the best way to clean your shower door's tracks, we've got it right here. First spray the inside of the tracks with your favorite bathroom cleaner, and let it sit for a few minutes to loosen the dirt and mildew. Then wrap a rag or paper towel around the pointed end of a screwdriver and use it to scrub the inside of the tracks. Rinse with water, and marvel at the results!

Simply Clean Tiles For an easy, natural tile cleaner, mix together ¼ cup baking soda and a gallon of warm water. Scrub with a sponge or mop, then rinse. For tough stains, wait 10 to 15 minutes before rinsing.

Beat Bathtub Ring The grimy ring around the bathtub is one of the most dreaded and persistent enemies in the fight between clean and evil. That potent mixture of dead skin cells, body grease, oils, and soap has sticky superpowers on your tub's surface. Our advice? Instead of worrying about the bathtub ring after it's already pasted onto the tub, take this easy step to prevent it in the first place: Simply drop a bit of baby oil into the water at bath time. It will keep the water from clinging to the sides and send it down the drain instead.

Bathroom Quick Clean Trying to clean up your bathroom fast, before guests arrive? Here's how to do it in two minutes or less: Apply a touch of baby shampoo to a wet sponge and wipe down your sink, fixtures, tiles, and bathtub. It cuts through oily residue, and it smells good too.

Pumice for Porcelain If you have a porcelain sink, you know that it can be very prone to scratches. Eliminate them with a pumice stone. First, fill the sink with water and add the pumice stone. Allow it to soak for a few minutes to get completely wet (if not, the stone could cause additional scratches), then begin to scrub until the scratches are removed. This tip works best on small scratches, not deep ones.

Who Knew? Classic Tip

If mineral deposits have built up in your sink's faucet, cut a lemon into quarters, then push one piece up into the faucet until it sticks. Leave for about 10 minutes, then twist the wedge out. Repeat with remaining lemon quarters until the deposits are gone.

Get Out of a Sticky Situation If you've ever had a shower curtain liner that kept sticking to you while you were trying to shower, you know it's less funny, more annoying. Get rid of this problem forever with a spray bottle! Pour a tablespoon of liquid fabric softener into it and fill the rest with water. Spray on the liner just before you shower and it will always stay in its proper place.

Streak-Free Mirrors If you've ever noticed streaks on your bathroom mirror the day after you clean it, you'll love this tip. When cleaning the bathroom, always wear a dark shirt. Streaks are much easier to spot when the mirror is reflecting something dark.

Get Rid of Caked-On Hair Spray If your beauty routine includes spraying your entire 'do to keep it in place, you probably have a film of hair spray on your bathroom vanity and walls. Remove it easily with a solution of two parts water and one part liquid fabric softener. Wipe on with a damp cloth, then rub off with a clean one.

Who Knew? Classic Tip

For a cheap and easy way to clean your toilet, use mouthwash. Just pour 1 capful into the bowl, leave for 10 to 15 minutes, and wipe clean with your toilet brush.

Mirror Makeover For a unique cleaner for the mirrors around your home, use aerosol air freshener. It will bring your mirrors to a glossy shine and will have people wondering where that flowery scent is coming from.

Sweeping and Vacuming

Neat Sweeping Tip Keep your dust where it belongs—in the dustpan—by spraying the pan with water before sweeping. That way, the dust will stick to the pan instead of falling back on the floor again.

Who Knew? Classic Tip

To eliminate the trail of dust your broom leaves behind, fill a spray bottle with three parts water and one part liquid fabric softener, and spray the broom before sweeping. The spritz makes the broom strands more pliable and helps it collect dirt more efficiently.

Clever Broom Storage Spot Need a convenient, yet out-of-the-way spot to store a broom? Magnetic tape can help. Just place a few pieces of magnetic tape on the brush handle, then stick it to the side of something metal, like your refrigerator.

Jailbreak Your Swiffer Did you know that you can refill a Swiffer Wetjet with your favorite cleaning product and avoid shelling out a lot of cash for the name-brand refills? To do this, you'll need a pot of boiling water, an empty Swiffer bottle, and nail clippers. Stick the top of the bottle in the boiling water for a minute or so, until the plastic becomes pliable. Using a towel to protect your hands, start turning the cap until it comes off. The heat should make it easy to remove. If not, use a nail clipper to clip away the plastic claws holding the bottle shut. Then dilute whichever cleaning product you plan to use, add it to the bottle, and reseal.

Rehab an Old Broom If your broom's bristles are sticking out every which way and you're thinking of replacing it, try this trick first. Place a rubber band at the bottom (along the bristles) and leave it for a few days. The band will realign the bristles, and it will sweep more effectively.

Ditch Split Ends To give new life to your dust mop, try giving it a trim! Frayed cotton strands don't pick up dirt well, so if you simply cut off those split ends with some scissors, your mop will be as effective as the day you bought it!

When Your Vacuum Stops Sucking Your DustBuster doesn't seem to be busting dust as well as it used to. The problem may be static buildup in the canister. Solve the problem with a dryer sheet! Cut off a piece of dryer sheet, vacuum it up, and allow the DustBuster to run for 30 to 60 seconds. Remove the sheet, and the vacuum should really, well, suck again!

Who Knew? Classic Tip

Just because you have a wet/dry mop like a Swiffer doesn't mean you have to spend a cent on those pricey replacement cloths! Instead, use a large sock from your "missing mates" pile and stretch it around the head of the mop. It will work just as well, and you can throw it in the washing machine when you're done!

De-Crud the Vacuum Is the roller on your vacuum cleaner all stopped up with hair, dust, string, and lint? Slice the culprits with a seam ripper to remove them easily (no tugging!), and the vacuum will be back at full power in no time.

Avoid Vacuuming Mistakes You can prevent marks on baseboards and walls when you vacuum by covering the edges of the vacuum head with masking tape so you don't leave behind dark smudges from the metal when you inevitably bump the wall.

Who Knew? Classic Tip

If your disposable vacuum cleaner bag is full and you don't have a replacement on hand, get out the duct tape! Remove the bag and cut a slit straight down the middle. Empty it into the garbage, then pinch the sides together at the slit and fold over. Tape the fold with a liberal amount of duct tape. The bag will hold a little less, but you'll be ready to vacuum again without having to run to the store.

Protect Your Vacuum Items like nails, staples, and even paper clips can harm your vacuum cleaner if they get sucked into the bag. Keep it safe from harm with a magnet and our old household friend duct tape. Just duct tape a strong magnet to the end of the hose and it will grab any small metal pieces before your vacuum can.

Battle Dust Bunnies The easiest way to vacuum under a dresser? Just remove the bottom drawer, and you'll be able to suck up those dust bunnies with ease.

DIY Vacuum Attachment Trying to clean super-small spaces around the house? Don't buy additional vacuum equipment if your attachments are too big. Instead, grab a straw—preferably one of those giant straws from a fast-food chain—and insert part of it into the smallest attachment you have. Tape it in place, and you'll be able to suck up dirt and dust in the tiniest of spaces.

Clean the Floor with Club Soda If you have some left-over club soda after a party, did you know that you can mop your tile floor with it? The carbonation in the club soda will help dissolve dirt. Just pour into a pail and use it like you would a mild soap solution.

Who Knew? Classic Tip

To rid your house of pet, cooking, or other smells, add a cotton ball soaked in vanilla or lavender oil to your vacuum cleaner bag. It's a great way to rid your home of an offensive odor by creating a nice scent instead.

Shine Your Wood Keep your hardwood floors looking their best with black tea! Put 1 quart boiling water into a bucket with several bags of black tea. Allow the mixture to steep for 10 minutes, then remove the bags. Lightly dampen a cloth with the mixture and rub it on the floor. When it dries, wash the floor as usual to reveal an amazing shine.

See Also . . . Fighting a stubborn carpet stain? Head to the Stain Solutions and Laundry Tips chapter.

Surprising Furniture Cleaners

Give Old Wood New Life We love the antique look of old wooden furniture. But sometimes "old" just looks, well, old rather than "antique." To get wood gleaming again, we've found that this easy trick is amazingly effective, and you only need two items that you probably already have in your kitchen: oil and vinegar. Yep, like the salad dressing! Mix ¼ cup white or apple-cider vinegar with ¾ cup cooking oil. Dip a soft cloth in the solution and start wiping!

Sofa Spruce-Up Upholstered sofas and chairs often get a musty odor from day-to-day wear, especially if your kids and pets romp around in the cushions. For a simple freshening up, sprinkle a bit of baking soda over the

who knew? THE BIG QUESTION

Cleaning Blinds

OK, so I've decided to tackle cleaning all of the blinds in my house today. Any tips?

—Chelsea Whitman, via Twitter

The Best Way to Clean Blinds One of our least favorite household chores has to be cleaning mini-blinds. Make the job faster and easier by donning a pair of old cotton gloves and using your gloved hands to dust. You can dust both sides of a slat at once, and then toss the gloves in the wash when you're done. (This is a great tip for those orphan gloves and mittens you discover in the back of the closet!)

Help Mini-Blinds Repel Dust To keep blinds clean longer, wipe them down with a mixture of one part fabric softener to three parts water. The fabric softener will repel dust, so you won't have to repeat this thankless task for a while!

Clean the Pull Cord To clean filthy pull cords on your blinds, get a stepladder or something the same height as the top of the blinds (where the pull cord begins). Fill a jar with cold water and add a tablespoon of bleach. Pull your blinds up so the maximum amount of cord possible is exposed. Rest the jar on top of the ladder and soak the cord for two to three hours. When you're done, transfer the cord to a jar of water to rinse, then pat dry with some rags or towels.

upholstery, between and underneath the cushions. Let sit for a few hours or up to a day, then suck up the remaining soda and debris with a vacuum.

Zap Fabric Odors To freshen up fabric and upholstery, you don't have to buy a bottle of chemical-filled commercial deodorizer. Just mix together 1 cup vodka and 1 cup water in a spray bottle, and spritz away. Then let sit for several minutes until the mixture evaporates. The ethanol in vodka helps zap unpleasant odors, and once it evaporates it will be odorless!

Who Knew? Classic Tip

You just bought the coffee table of your dreams, but when it was sitting in the store you didn't realize it would attract fingerprints like bees to honey. To get rid of a persistent fingerprint problem, rub down the tabletop with cornstarch. The surface will absorb the cornstarch, which will repel prints.

Nail Polish Stain? Spill nail polish on wood furniture or floors? Do not reach for the polish remover, which can leave even uglier stains on wood. Instead, grab a bottle of hair spray and apply generously over your polish stain, leave for 20 seconds, and wipe away. Repeat as many times as it takes to abolish the polish! Hair spray works wonderfully on clothes and carpets too, although you should always test a patch before you treat the material.

Help with Pet Hair It's great to have your cat or dog curled up next to you on the couch while you watch the game, but not so much fun to get his hair off of it and other pieces of furniture. To easily remove pet hair, make this magic pet-hair remover: Mix 1 part liquid fabric softener with 2 parts water in a spray bottle. Then spritz your furniture before vacuuming. The hairs will adhere to the softener, making them much easier to remove. As an added benefit, the room will smell fresh and clean!

Who Knew? Classic Tip

If you have a mark on your wood furniture or floor that won't come off with furniture polish, try leaving mayonnaise on the stain for an hour, then wiping off.

How to Clean Microfiber Microfiber furniture looks beautiful and elegant thanks to its tiny, shiny fibers that can resemble suede or leather. The big downside: It can be hard to clean. Check the tag on your microfiber item. If there's a "W" on the tag, you can go ahead and use water and soap to clean it; if there's an "S," you'll need to use a solvent-based cleaner, because even water could stain the fabric. If you have an "S," here's what to do: First, vacuum the area using a soft-brush attachment to suck up any dirt and debris. Then spray rubbing alcohol over the soiled area using a spray bottle. Scrub using a rough sponge or old toothbrush, and the stains will lift right off. The fabric should dry quickly, but if it seems hardened or discolored afterward, simply stroke it with a toothbrush or soft scrub brush until it's back to its velvety form.

Easy Ceiling Fan Clean Some may say that opening an umbrella in the house is bad luck, but you won't mind the risk when you see how much easier it makes cleaning your ceiling fan. Just hook the handle of an upside-down, open umbrella over the top of the fan, then let the dust that you wipe off the blades fall inside. Close it up when you're done and carefully take outside to dump the dust out.

Mattress Freshener It's easy to toss bed sheets and mattress covers in the wash, but the mattress itself can be trickier to keep clean. To freshen up and kill any foul odors on your mattress, add a tablespoon each of liquid fabric softener and baking soda to a spray bottle filled with water, and spritz the mixture on your mattress. Your mattress will smell better than new!

Bed Pillow Know-How Here's an easy way to start your spring-cleaning: Begin with your bed pillows. To make them fluffy and fresh, just place them in the clothes dryer with fabric softener and two clean tennis balls for a few minutes.

Quick Cleans for Household Objects

Clean Out Keyboard Crud Eating at the computer is a popular habit in our house—and we are all guilty of it! If your keyboard is littered with crumbs, dirt, and dust between the keys, here's an easy cleaning trick: Use a short strip of tape to clean out the crud. Just press the tape between and underneath the keys so the dirt sticks, then toss it.

Cleaning Battery Leaks If battery acid leaks inside the compartments of your appliances, there's no need to throw them away. Simply take few spoonfuls of baking soda and add water until it's the consistency of toothpaste. Spread it on your battery terminals, let it sit 15 minutes, and wipe clean. The acid should come off easily.

Clean a Steamer with H_2O_2 To give the inside of your humidifier or steamer an easy clean, combine 1 pint hydrogen peroxide with 1 gallon water and pour into the tank. Run the machine as you normally would, and it'll be squeaky clean in no time.

Who Knew? Classic Tip

Save plastic squeeze bottles, but not for storage—they make the perfect substitute for bottles of compressed air, which are used to clean out computer keyboards, electronics, and other tiny crevices. This works especially well with squeeze bottles with small spouts, such as lemon juice dispensers. Wash them well and let them dry completely before using.

Cleaning Clay Your child made an amazing clay pot or figurine in art class, but you're afraid of cleaning it because clay can be so fragile. Here's how to do it: Fill a bowl with warm water and add a couple of tablespoons of baking soda. Mix until the baking soda dissolves, then add the clay item and let sit for 1 hour. Rinse thoroughly and dry immediately for super-clean clay!

Coin Cleaning If you collect coins, you'll love this trick for keeping them looking shiny and new. In a small bowl, mix together ¼ cup white vinegar with 1½ teaspoons salt. Place your coins into the mixture, wait a few minutes, then drain and dry them. Buff with a dry cloth and a little bit of oil. They'll look as good as the day they were minted!

Who Knew? Classic Tip

To clean stuffed animals, just place them in a cloth bag or pillowcase, add baking soda or cornmeal, and shake. The dirt will transfer to the powder.

Photo Fixer Smudges and fingerprints on photos can be hard to remove, but witch hazel makes it easy! Found in the beauty section of most drugstores, this astringent helps lift stains and evaporate oily residue. Just dampen a paper towel or clean rag with the witch hazel and gently rub the photo until the spot disappears. Let air dry before putting back in an album or frame.

THE BIG QUESTION who knew?

Candle Cleaning

How do I get wax off of candlesticks?

—Katrina Ortiz, via WhoKnewTips.com

What is the easiest way to clean a decorative candle? **—Elizabeth Donnellon, via Facebook**

Wax Off To remove small bits of wax stuck to candlesticks, there's an easy fix: Just run them under hot water. The heat will melt the remaining wax, so you can wipe it away.

Get Rid of Waxy Buildup If your candleholder has some wax buildup, stop trying to scrape it off with your fingernail and head to the kitchen. Mix olive oil with dish soap in equal parts, wipe onto candlestick, and let sit for 5 minutes. Then rub off with a dry cloth. The wax should come with it!

Prevent Wax from Sticking To prevent wax from sticking to a candleholder in the first place, rub a thin coat of olive oil on the base of the holder before lighting the candle.

Quick Candle Clean Decorative candles add a beautiful touch to your home, until they get dusty! To easily get them clean, grab an old pair of nylons. Rubbing the candle with the nylons provides the perfect amount of friction to get the dirt off without harming the candle's surface.

Surprising Brass Cleaner Shine doorknobs, candlesticks, or anything else brass with Worcestershire sauce! Use a few drops on a damp cloth to rub brass clean. You won't believe how shiny it gets until you try it!

Ketchup for Copper Here's an unlikely cleaning tool—ketchup. It works great on copper. Simply rub on with a soft cloth, let sit for 30 to 45 minutes, then rinse off with hot water and wipe dry.

Who Knew? Classic Tip

Before cleaning the ashes from your fireplace, sprinkle some damp coffee grounds over them. They'll weigh the ashes down and keep dust to a minimum.

Citrus for Ceramic To clean dust off ceramic figurines, simply rub them with the cut side of a lemon wedge. Leave the lemon juice on for 15 minutes, then polish up with a soft, dry cloth.

How to Clean Golf Clubs By now you've probably realized that we have a substitution for just about every household cleaner. But what about when your prized golf clubs get dirty? Resist the urge to spend money on fancy cleaners. Instead, dissolve a scoop of laundry detergent into a bucket of water, and soak your clubs for one minute (no longer). The detergent has the exact same ingredients as those expensive club cleaners.

No More Musty Books If you're placing some old books in storage and don't want them to acquire a musty smell, here's the solution. Place a new sheet of fabric softener inside the pages, and that battered copy of *To Kill a Mockingbird* will stay nice and fresh until you need it again. If you fail to follow this tip or if you have books that are *already* musty, just place them in a paper grocery bag with an open box of baking soda. Fold over the bag, staple it shut, and let it sit for a week or two. Your books should smell considerably better when you take them out.

How to Easily Clean a Dirty Radiator Dreading cleaning your radiator? Here's a simple way to get the job done. Hang a damp cloth or damp newspapers on the wall behind it, then use your hair dryer to blow the dust off it. The dust will stick to the wet surface behind it, and then you can simply throw away the cloth or paper.

chapter 7

Stain Solutions and Laundry Tips

Getting Rid of Stubborn Carpet Stains

Removing Clothing Stains

De-Wrinkling Wonders

Making Clothes Last Longer

Laundry Problems, Solved

Cleaning Shoes and Accessories

Getting Rid of Stubborn Carpet Stains

Cast Out Carpet Stains Notice a new spot on the carpet? Don't panic: There's no need to hire a professional carpet cleaner just yet. Just combine equal amounts of hot water and ammonia and pour over the stain. Place a white towel on top, then iron over the covered spot. The cleaning powers of ammonia combined with the extreme heat will steam out the stain in no time!

Removing Ink Stains Ink stains on the carpet? Make a paste of cream of tartar and lemon juice, and dab at the stain. Let it sit for five minutes or so, then clean with a damp cloth.

Coffee Cleanup Get rid of coffee stains with one of our favorite household helpers: vinegar. Blot the stain with a solution of one part vinegar and one part water, then let sit for 10 minutes. If it's a tablecloth or piece of clothing, wash in the washing machine as usual. If it's carpet, then dab with a clean paper towel and repeat with the vinegar mixture until the stain is lifted.

A Carpet Conundrum The kids were out playing in the mud, and—lucky you—they forgot to take off their shoes before traipsing on the carpet. Don't worry; it's not impossible to get rid of those muddy footprints. First, let the area dry, and vacuum up as much dirt as you can. Then, using the cut side of a raw potato, rub the stains. The enzymes in the potato will help dissolve the dirt. Allow the area to dry again, and then blot with a wet rag.

Who Knew? Classic Tip

If you spill any liquid on your carpet, pour salt on the area as soon as possible and watch it absorb the liquid almost instantly. Wait until it dries, then vacuum it up. Salt tends to provide a special capillary attraction that will work for most liquids. There are a few stains that salt will actually help set, however—never sprinkle it on red wine, coffee, tea, or cola!

Less Yuck If you have kids, you've had to clean up vomit. Baking soda can make the job a little less gross if you sprinkle some on top as soon as possible. It will soak up some of the mess and make the smell easier to deal with when you have to go at it with the paper towels.

Removing Red Wine What's the easiest way to remove red wine spills from your carpet? Try applying a bit of shaving cream (after checking that the carpet is colorfast) for a minute. Or try our go-to stain remover: a spray bottle with a mixture of half hydrogen peroxide, half Dawn dishwashing liquid.

Removing Clothing Stains

When Stains Are a Pain Forget expensive stain pretreatments for your laundry—just reach for the baby shampoo! Use just as you would a pretreater and it will work just as well for a fraction of the cost.

Iron Away Chocolate Stains Who knew your iron could help you remove chocolate stains? First, allow the stain to dry and gently scrape off what you can with a spoon. Then cover the stain with a paper towel, and turn your iron on low. By ironing over the paper towel, the chocolate will melt again and transfer to the towel. Then launder your item as usual.

Make a Bleach Pen Bleach pens can be a godsend for laundry stains. But for a fraction of the price of those you

who knew? THE BIG QUESTION

Removing Grease Stains

How do you get a grease stain out of clothes? **—Pete Reidy, via Facebook**

Grease Grabber Like most stains, the sooner you can get at grease stains, the better. If possible, start as soon as the stain starts! Blot with a paper towel to remove any excess grease, then cover the area with talcum, baby, or baking powder. Don't be shy here—you really want to coat the stains. The powder will absorb the grease. Wait a few hours before shaking it off and you might not even need a pre-treater before washing as usual.

Grease Be Gone! You rely on dishwashing liquid to remove grease from your dishes and pans. Why not try it on your clothes as well? Rub a little dishwashing liquid into the grease stain, then launder as usual.

A Stain Remover on Your Table If you drop greasy food on your clothes while you're out at a restaurant, don't dab with water or club soda, which can simply spread the oily stain. Instead, blot it up with an artificial sweetener like Equal. Its super-absorbent granules will soak up most of the stain before you even get home!

find at the store, you can make a do-it-yourself version. All you need are a few ingredients you probably already have on hand. Grab a small squeeze bottle with a narrow dispensing hole at the top, cornstarch, and bleach. In a small pan, combine ½ cup cold water and 1 tablespoon cornstarch. Stir until the cornstarch is combined. Bring the mixture to a boil, so that the cornstarch thickens, then remove from the heat. Once it's cool, stir in 2 to 3 tablespoons bleach, and transfer the mixture to a squeeze container. To use, squeeze out a little bit on your worst stains and spots!

Who Knew? Classic Tip

Don't let a stain "set" even if you are running out the door. Instead, spray with stain remover or soak in water and store in a resealable plastic bag until you have time to deal with it. Once a stain dries, it's much harder to remove.

Lift Up Mud Stains Have the kids come home with fresh mud stains on their clothes? Don't apply water! Instead, let the mud dry, then use a piece of packing or duct tape to lift up all of the hardened dirt you can. Then wash as usual.

Lather Up Those Stains Did you know that shaving cream can remove stains? The alcohols in the cream help eliminate the offending spots. So the next time a little ketchup or jam falls on your clothes, dampen the area with cold water and rub in a little shaving cream. Wait 5 to 10 minutes, then wash as usual.

Who Knew? Classic Tip

To get juice stains off of your clothes, just use boiling water. Hold the garment over the tub and very carefully pour boiling water through the fabric where the stain is. It will remove the stain without you having to put your clothes through the hot cycle in the washing machine.

Try Toothpaste for Drink Stains Get rid of wine and coffee stains on clothes with toothpaste! Massage a little of the white (not gel) variety into the stains, then rinse and repeat if needed.

Berry Stain? If you accidentally got berry juice on your clothes, soak the stain overnight in equal parts milk and white vinegar. Then launder as usual.

Get the Grass Out A long day of outdoor play left your child's jeans covered in grass stains at the knees. Remove the stains by soaking the jeans in a mixture of half hydrogen peroxide, half water for 30 minutes, before rinsing and laundering as usual. Hydrogen peroxide is a gentle bleaching agent that helps to loosen stains in fabric.

Stick It to a Pollen Stain Out smelling the flowers and now have a pollen stain on your shirt? Don't rub at it! Carefully shake off the excess pollen and then remove the rest with a piece of masking or duct tape.

Who Knew? Classic Tip

If your dress shirts are getting stained around the collar, wipe the back of your neck with an alcohol-based astringent before you get dressed in the morning. The alcohol will prevent your sweat from leaving a stain.

Goodbye to Underarm Stains The easiest way to remove yellow underarm stains is with a 50/50 mix a spray bottle of hydrogen peroxide and Dawn dishwashing liquid. Just spray it on the stain, add a little baking soda, and scrub away. Launder as usual and your shirts will be white again!

Relief from Stains Blood and sweat stains are two of the toughest to get out, so get a little help from something that's tough on heartburn: Alka-Seltzer! Just pop two into a pot of cool water and add the stained item. Let sit for a half hour before washing and the Alka-Seltzer's bubbles and active ingredients will lift stains from fibers.

Get Rid of Gas Stains Removing gasoline stains from clothing can be tricky. The most effective way we know of is to apply baby oil to the stain, then launder as usual. Since gasoline is an oil-based product, it takes another oil to pull out the stain and smell.

Tackling Tar Stains If you have a tar stain on your clothes, try petroleum jelly—just rub it in until the tar is gone. The jelly itself might stain the fabric, but it's easy to remove with a spray-and-wash stain remover.

Fix a Makeup Mishap If you've stained your towels or clothes with foundation, eye shadow, or blush, you don't have to leave your bathroom to get it out. Dampen the stain with water, rub gently with a white bar soap (like Dove or Ivory), then rinse well and throw in with the rest of your laundry.

Lipstick Lifter Lipstick can be one of hardest stains to remove—if you don't use the right stain remover. The grease in lipstick makes it hard to get out of the fibers in fabric, but rubbing alcohol breaks through it nicely. Just apply rubbing alcohol with a damp cloth to the stain, and dab until the lipstick starts to come off, applying more alcohol as necessary. Then launder as usual.

Who Knew? Classic Tip

If you have a scorch mark on fabric, your quest to remove it begins in the kitchen. Cut the end off of an onion and grate about a fourth of it into a bowl using a cheese grater. Rub the stain with the grated onion, blotting it with as much of the onion juice as you can. Let it sit for 8 to 10 minutes, and if necessary, re-apply the onion juice. Once the stain is gone, launder as usual.

Solve a Suntan-Oil Spill You had a great time at the beach, but you accidentally got suntan lotion all over your cover-up. To remove this stubborn stain, cover with liquid dish detergent and rub in. Then turn your kitchen sink on at full blast and run under cold water.

Pummel Marker Stains Yes, there's even hope for permanent marker stains, and it comes in the form of something you already have in your bag: hand sanitizer. Squirt it around the edges of the stains and then work your way in, then let sit for five minutes (fabrics) to 10 minutes (hard surfaces like countertops) before cleaning. Just make sure you test the material for color-fastness, as hand sanitizer can discolor it.

Ink Answers Trying to get an ink stain out? Spray ultra-stiffening hair spray on the spot, then launder as usual. Hair spray will usually remove the stain.

De-Wrinkling Wonders

Pant Wrinkles, Solved Drying wet pants by hanging them over a hanger is convenient, but can often lead to a giant wrinkle where you folded them over. Solve this problem forever with a paper towel tube! Cut a slit down it (lengthwise), slide it over the "bar" of the hanger, and hold in place with strong tape. When you hang pants over the tube, its gentle curve will keep them from wrinkling!

De-Wrinkling Silk It can be tough to get wrinkles out of delicate silk blouses, since it's usually not safe to use your iron's steam setting on them. Instead, use an ice cube wrapped in a washcloth. Rub it on any wrinkles, then iron on the lowest heat setting. It's damp enough to help flatten the fabric without being too hot to handle.

Who Knew? Classic Tip

Need to wash your sheer curtains but hate the thought of ironing them? Simply dissolve a packet of clear gelatin in the final rinse when laundering, and hang them up damp afterward. The gelatin will remove almost all the wrinkles.

For Wrinkle-Free Sheets Though we like wrinkle-free linens as much as the next person, we simply don't have the time to iron bed sheets like our mothers used to. Still, there are a few things you can do to stop wrinkles before they start. Believe it or not, drying your sheets in the dryer can actually increase and set wrinkles. Instead, fold the sheet into quarters or eighths, snapping it and smoothing it out after each fold. Then place the last fold over a clothesline. The fabric is so light, it will easily dry, with only a few wrinkles still intact.

Wrinkle Reliever Want to get wrinkles out of a shower curtain, drapes, or something else so large it's bulky to iron? Try using your hair dryer instead. Set it on the highest setting and gently run over the hanging fabric. It's quicker and easier than getting out the ironing board.

Who Knew? Classic Tip

Covering your ironing board with shiny-side-up foil before you iron your clothes will get them unwrinkled twice as fast, saving you time and energy!

Spray Wrinkles Away! Now you can remove wrinkles in your clothes without breaking out the ironing board—or paying for one of those wrinkle-releaser sprays. Just use this easy recipe for a homemade version: In a spray bottle, combine equal amounts of apple cider vinegar, fabric softener, and water. Gently mist over the any wrinkles and creases, then smooth out the wrinkles while holding the garment slightly taut while it's still damp.

Dry Delicates Faster After hand-washing clothes they can stay damp for hours, but trying to wring them out can leave huge wrinkles. Solve this problem with a rolling pin and two towels. Fold the towels and place your wet garment between them. Then roll the rolling pin over the towels several times to get out the water five times faster than air-drying alone.

Make Your Iron Grime-Free Sticky iron? Solve it with a used fabric softener sheet placed on top of your ironing board. Just set the iron on medium with no steam, then iron the dryer sheet until the stickiness is gone. The grime will stick to the sheet for easy disposal!

Iron on Your Favorite Fragrance This smart tip will make your clothes smell wonderful. Add a drop of perfume to the water in your steam iron, then iron your shirts, underwear, lingerie—everything! You'll enjoy your favorite perfume wherever you go.

Making Clothes Last Longer

Lemon for Your Laundry Dulling colors got you down? You can bring your lackluster whites back to sparkling with ¼ to ½ cup lemon juice added to the wash cycle. No bleach necessary!

The Dirt on Dirty Laundry You likely already sort your laundry by color and wash cycle, but did you know you should also sort by how dirty the clothes are? Make sure to wash heavily soiled items separately because the dirt that they release in the wash can be picked up by less dirty clothes.

Who Knew? Classic Tip

The easiest way to make your clothes last longer is to wash them less. Many of your clothes can be worn several times before you wash them, especially sweaters. Most items get more wear and tear from being in the washing machine than they do on your bodies! When you do throw in a load, make sure to turn knitted clothes and T-shirts with designs on them inside out when washing and drying.

Washer Advice It might seem more cost-effective to stuff your washing machine to the brim, but it's actually less efficient—the clothes rub against each other more, and the water doesn't have as much room to flush away dirt and oils. For the best wash, only fill your washing machine three-quarters full. This gives your clothes enough room to get fully clean.

Don't Toss That Snagged Swimwear! You might know that clear nail polish will stop a run in stockings, but did you know it will also work on snagged swimwear? Paint a little bit on the run, and check periodically before hitting the pool to see if it needs a touch-up.

Who Knew? Classic Tip

Rotate through your bras rather than wear one for a few days in a row. You'll give the elastic time to contract and the bras will last longer. Who knew?

Breathe Easier After the Dry Cleaner It's tempting to leave freshly dry-cleaned items in the plastic bags that the clothes are returned to you in. After all, it seems like they'll stay cleaner longer that way. But the truth is that those bags can trap perchloroethylene—a toxic solvent used in dry cleaning—in the fabric. The fix is simple: Just remove the bags and hang the clothes outside or in the garage for an hour or two before returning them to your closet. The chemical will vaporize, and you'll breathe easier.

Freeze Your Jeans It sounds crazy, but you can save wear and tear on your jeans by cutting down on the number of times you put them through the washing machine—freeze them instead! The freezer eliminates many of the same odors and bacteria as the washing machine, so you can cut down on how often you wash your jeans, thus making the fabric last longer. Just shake off any debris, fold the jeans neatly, and put them in a plastic bag. Place in the freezer overnight, and in the morning, they'll be ready to wear. (Of course, you'll need to toss them into the washer for a periodic freshening up, and to remove stains.)

Safe Storage for Your Clothes When storing your winter clothes for the season, don't place them in an airtight container, which will trap moisture inside and can lead to mildew spores forming. Instead, use an old duffel bag or suitcase. If you don't have one available, wrap your clothes in a large sheet and knot it at the top.

Don't Button Up When you wash button-down shirts and polos, make sure to unbutton them before tossing in the machine. The agitation can weaken the threads and increase the chance that the buttons will loosen or fall off.

Restore Velvet If your velvet dress, shawl, shirt, or pants are getting a shiny mark from too much wear, you may be able to remove it. Try lightly spraying the area with water, then rubbing against the grain with an old toothbrush.

Laundry Problems, Solved

Sock Mystery Solved! Tired of losing socks every time you do the laundry? We are too! To prevent your footsies from doing a washing-machine disappearing act, secure sock pairs together with binder clips. Instead of knocking your socks off, you'll be keeping them on! (Sorry, we couldn't resist!)

Keep Jeans from Shrinking Jeans are usually tight enough as it is! To minimize shrinking, wash them in cold water, dry them on medium heat for only 10 minutes, and then air-dry them the rest of the way.

Eliminate Smells in Mildewed Laundry It's happened to the best of us—you accidentally left your laundry in the washing machine and now it smells like a mildewy mess. To get your clothes smelling fresh again, leave them in the washing machine and add a couple of cups of white vinegar and nothing else. Wash on the highest heat setting acceptable for your clothes; when it's finished, wash them again using your regular laundry detergent. Then dry on the highest heat setting possible until completely dry (the heat should kill any remaining mildew). If the laundry still smells funky when it's completely dry, try this intense overnight soak: Place it back in the washing machine and stop the cycle once the machine is filled with just enough water to cover the clothes (again, use the hottest water possible). Add 1 cup ammonia and stir to distribute thoroughly into the water; let soak overnight. The next morning, add detergent (make sure it's one with no bleach added), continue the wash cycle, and dry in the dryer again. By now, you should be able to say farewell to the funky smell!

A Dryer-Sheet Alternative Out of dryer sheets on laundry day? No problem! Try using aluminum foil instead: Just crumple a strip of foil into a ball and toss it in the dryer with your laundry. Not only does it eliminate static, the tin foil is reusable for future loads.

Who Knew? Classic Tip

Add a big, dry towel to the clothes dryer when drying jeans and other bulky items. It will cut the drying time significantly.

Static Cure Slinky skirt grabbing your pantyhose and won't let go? Solve this annoyance with an unlikely household hero: a battery! Just rub the positive end of a battery over your skirt and hose. (If this happens to you a lot, you can just keep a AAA battery in your purse!) The battery releases positively charged ions that neutralize the negative ones that cause static cling. Bada-bing, no more static cling!

Who Knew? Classic Tip

Line-drying your clothes is energy efficient and great for them. Not only is air-drying less harsh, you'll also love the real smell of sun-dried linens. If you don't have a clothesline, hang shirts and pants on hangers from tree limbs! Just make sure not to put brights in the sun, as they made fade.

An Ace of a Dryer Tip To reduce static cling naturally, toss a few (clean!) tennis balls into your dryer with your laundry. Tumble dry on low heat. The balls will bounce around, keeping clothes from sticking together.

Make a Laundry List Make laundry a little easier by making an easier reminder of items that you can throw into the washer to make a full load. All of us have items that we only need to wash every once in a while, whether it's a throw for the couch, a shower curtain, or a bedspread. Do an inventory of those items in your house and post the list in your laundry room. Then, the next time you have a

THE BIG QUESTION who knew?

Stale-Smelling Towels

Even right after I wash them, my towels still have an "off" smell that I can't get rid of!! What should I do so I don't have to buy all new towels? **—Elena Osborne Gonzalez, via Facebook**

Tackling Towel Trouble If a regular wash cycle is futile against your stale-smelling towels, it's probably due to mildew. Towels are frequently damp for extended periods of time, which makes them an easy breeding ground for bacteria and fungi—hence the musty, sour odor. Now that you're properly disgusted, it's time to take action against those nasty culprits! Get your towels into fresh form with a simple mixture of hydrogen peroxide and vinegar. Combine equal parts of each in a bucket, then let the towels soak in the mixture for 15 minutes before washing as usual in the washing machine.

Calling in the Big Guns Do your towels *still* smell musty and stale? Try this: Wash the towels with your regular detergent on the highest heat allowed on the tag, then add a cup of ammonia during the rinse cycle. Wash again without the ammonia, then dry on the highest heat possible or line-dry in the sun. Make sure the towels are completely dry before storing away! To keep the smell from starting in the first place, try to line-dry towels in a sunny, warm spot whenever possible.

smallish load, check your list and add one of those items to the wash. (You can even note on your list the date that you washed it.) You'll make more efficient use of your washing machine—and you'll ensure that those easy-to-forget things are always clean.

Less Expensive Laundry Gizmo The secret, low-cost alternative to one of those balls that releases fabric softener during your laundry load? A clean kitchen sponge dampened with liquid fabric softener. Just put it in the washing machine once it's filled with water at the beginning of the load. It will slowly release the softener, just like the plastic balls do!

Quick Lint Disposal Here's a clever way to get rid of dryer lint: Stick an empty tissue box near your washer and dryer, and simply tuck the lint inside after scooping it out of the dryer. The plastic-lined opening of the tissue box keeps lint from flying away! When the box is full, trash it, use the lint as compost, or toss it into a campfire—lint is a first-rate fire starter.

Laundry Slam Dunk Turn a drawstring laundry bag into an ingenious hanging hamper with an old embroidery hoop. Just slip the opening of the bag through the hoop and it will stay open while you use the drawstrings to hang it from an over-the-door hook or in the closet. Bonus: It looks enough like a basketball hoop that it makes it a tiny bit easier to get our boys to straighten up their rooms!

Makeshift Clothesline If you need to air-dry delicates but don't have a clothesline, hang a long strand of dental floss and place lightweight clothes on it to dry. Floss is sturdy enough to hold underwear, bathing suits, and even tank tops and light T-shirts.

Who Knew? Classic Tip

Repurpose an old ice cube tray as an organizational tool for your laundry room. It's perfect for keeping buttons that have fallen off your clothes and other small items you may find in your pockets.

End Laundry Mayhem Has this conversation ever happened in your house? "Can this go in the dryer? What about this? Should I hang this up? What about that?" End it forever with a dry erase marker. When you put laundry in the washing machine, write what garments can't go in the dryer on the lid of the washer. Then erase it before your next load. Problem solved!

Cleaning Shoes and Accessories

The Ultimate Shoe Shine Get your rubber shoes back to squeaky-clean condition with this powerful all-purpose cleaning tool: the dishwasher! Add a bit of baking soda along with your usual dish detergent, and place flip-flops, Crocs, and even rubber boots in the machine for a hot wash alone without any dishes. Be sure to remove lining inserts and laces beforehand—laces can go into the regular washing machine and then hang to air-dry.

Who Knew? Classic Tip

To keep your shoes smelling better, store them in the freezer! It sounds funny, but it's true: The cold temperature slows down the growth of microscopic funkiness-makers.

Scrub Off Scuffs Just about any scuff mark can be removed with the help of some nail polish remover. Wet a rag with some, then rub on the scuff mark lightly but quickly. You may need to give your shoes the once-over with a damp cloth afterward.

Give Your Leather Some Love To remove dirt and make your leather goods shine, try cleaning them with egg whites. First beat together an egg white or two, and then rub it into the leather with a soft cloth. (Test first on an inconspicuous area.) Wipe the egg white away and buff with a clean cloth. You won't believe the results!

Who Knew? Classic Tip

To protect your leather shoes from getting damaged and stained by too much rock salt in the winter months, coat them with hair conditioner and let it soak in. The conditioner will repel the salt, and help keep the shoes supple.

Erase Pen Marks on Suede If you get a pen mark on your favorite suede handbag (or any other suede item), you probably think you'll have to live with it, but you just might rescue it with this tip. Take a brand-new pencil eraser, and rub it in the direction of the grain. The little particles that come off the eraser will get under the surface to remove to stain.

Stinky Sports Equipment? If you've got little linebackers, goalies, and sluggers in the family, you know how funky their equipment can get. Luckily, the dishwasher can work miracles on even the foulest sports gear. Toss kneepads, shin guards, and hockey pads into the top rack (with nothing else in the dishwasher!), squeeze some lemon juice into where you'd normally put the detergent, and run a normal wash cycle.

Just Don't Slip Here's an unlikely tool for polishing your shoes: a banana. Just rub the banana peel over your shoes, moist side down. Then buff with a soft cloth.

White Sneakers That Stay White After purchasing new white canvas sneakers, spray them with spray starch to help them resist stains. The starch will repel grease and dirt, keeping them whiter!

Who Knew? Classic Tip

Wash a baseball cap on the top rack of your dishwasher, and remove while still wet. Then, place the cap over a bowl to regain its shape, and dry it away from direct sunlight.

Jewelry Cleaner Baking soda is safe and effective when it comes to cleaning gold and silver jewelry. For best results, use a paste of baking soda and hydrogen peroxide, and rub gently on your jewelry. It gets rid of dirt, grime, and body oils, and leaves your gold and silver sparkling.

Get Sparkling Pearls with Vegetable Oil Because they're so fragile, pearls can't be cleaned with normal jewelry cleaners. Instead, use vegetable oil. Dab some oil on a soft cloth, then gently rub on each pearl. Let the vegetable oil dry overnight, then buff with a soft cloth to remove dust and oils that can make pearls look dull over time.

Special Stones Since turquoise, opals, and marcasite are porous stones, never immerse them in water. Instead, polish them with a soft, dry chamois.

Impromptu Glasses Cleaner The next time you're digging through your pockets looking for a cloth you can clean your glasses with, try a dollar bill. Press hard and it will do the job of a glasses cloth in a pinch.

Surprising Glasses Defogger Most optometrists will try to sell you an expensive cleaner when you buy your glasses. Instead of buying theirs, simply use a tiny dab of white toothpaste (not a gel) on both sides of the lenses to polish them and keep them from fogging up.

chapter 8

Keeping Away Clutter

Quick Household
Clutter-Busters

Kitchen Organizing Ideas

Bathroom Storage Solutions

Jewelry and Other Accessories

Crafty Craft and Hobby Storage

Closet Chaos Solved

Quick Household Clutter-Busters

Quick Cleanup Trick Company's coming over in a few minutes, and you need to clean up the living room pronto. Grab two plastic grocery bags, and try this tip. In one, place items to be thrown out. In the other, add items that don't belong in the room. Toss the trash, and then put the other things in their place.

Soap Dish Key Holder Tired of searching for your house keys every time you're getting ready to step out the door? Install a mountable soap dish on a wall near the entryway, and stick your keys in the dish when you enter the house. Problem solved!

On-the-Go at Your Front Door The entryway of our house is guaranteed to be littered with accessories all year round: gloves, scarves, and hats in the wintertime; sunglasses, sunscreen, and baseball caps in the summertime; house keys, gum, iPods, and cell phones all the time. That's why we love this easy idea for the foyer. Place a small galvanized tub or other container near the front door, and divide it into compartments using strips of cardboard or foam core—then stick your family's go-to on-the-go items inside.

Who Knew? Classic Tip

To store posters, certificates, degrees, and other valuable paper items, roll them up and pop them into a cardboard tube, like a toilet paper or paper towel roll. It will protect them from tears and creases and make them easier to tuck away.

Bag It! One of our favorite organizational tools is a hanging shoe organizer. These canvas contraptions are made to allow you to store your shoes on the back of a door, but their individualized compartments make them perfect for storing anything. Keep one in the bathroom for bobby pins, make-up, and lotion; one in your kitchen for spices; and one in the TV room for rarely used remotes and video game controllers. We also keep one in each of our children's rooms, so that when we yell, "Clean up your room!" they have a handy place to stow toy cars, action figures, and the million other little things that find their way onto their floors.

Bills, Bills, Bills Need one accessible spot to file your bills? Use a napkin holder! Even better, organize the bills by date so you know which ones should be paid first.

Revive Your Rolodex Still have that decades-old Rolodex from office jobs past? Rather than let it collect dust while you check your smartphone's address book, give it new life as a card organizer! Collect gift cards, store credit cards, and rewards cards in the circular file, and check it before you head out shopping or browse online stores. As a bonus, you'll also free up valuable space in your wallet. Win-win!

Who Knew? Classic Tip

Got an extra pot-lid rack sitting around? Use it as a mail sorter! Paint it first, if you like, then organize your mail by size from front to back—small items in the front (bills, postcards, letters) and larger ones (magazines and catalogs) in the back.

Set Up a Mail-Sorting System Is that ever-growing pile of mail giving you nightmares? Regain control by setting up this simple sorting system. As you open each piece of mail, stick it into one of the following designated files or letter boxes: "Follow Up," "Records," and "Review" (i.e., re-read). We also keep a small, inconspicuous trashcan near our usual mail-opening spot. That way, we can easily toss junk mail into the garbage without setting it on a table or countertop, where it will sit for weeks.

Make Your Own Mudroom Need a designated area where you and your kids can remove dirty shoes and damp clothing before sullying up your carpet? Turn a walk-in closet near the front door into a mudroom! Remove any items from the closet and install hooks on the walls that are reachable for small kids (if necessary). Place a large bin, several boxes, or a shoe rack on the floor, as well as shelves or containers for gloves and bags. If there's no convenient closet near the entryway, consider placing an armoire in the area: You can hang hooks on the doors and use the shelves and drawers to store the stinky outerwear.

Spare Furniture-Part Storage This tip solves two toolbox problems at once: The problem of not knowing what each of those tiny bags of parts goes with, and the problem of never being able to find the right ones when you need them. When a new piece of furniture comes with a bag of extra parts, tape it to the bottom or back of the furniture itself.

Gift-Wrap Protectors We love this trick for keeping rolls of wrapping paper intact and safe from creases and tears. Cut a slice through cardboard toilet paper tubes from top to bottom, then slip them around your wrapping paper roll. For slimmer rolls, tape the ends of the cardboard and adjust as needed. When you need some paper, simply remove the cardboard covers and you're ready to wrap!

Who Knew? Classic Tip

An empty tissue box is great for holding plastic shopping bags that are waiting for their chance at a second life. As you place each bag in the box, make sure its handles are poking up through the hole. Then thread each new bag through the previous bag's handles. That way, when you pull a bag out of the box, the next one will pop right up.

The Wire You just hit a big sale on wrapping paper, but now you don't know where to store it all. Be like Lionel Richie and head up toward the ceiling! Ceiling wrapping-paper storage is easier that you think. First, you'll need a space in your home like a closet or hallway, where two parallel walls are close together. A few inches from the ceiling, run several lengths of wire from these two walls, about four to six inches apart. The wires will form a simple

who knew? THE BIG QUESTION

Cords and Chargers

What's a good way to keep cell-phone chargers and other cords organized?

—Tracy Marques, via Facebook

Head to a Hardware Store A Kindle, an iPad, and a handful of cell phones: We have a similar cluster of electronics around our house! Here's the solution we used for neatening things up a bit: foam pipe insulation from the hardware store. (It usually has a lengthwise slit in it; if not, cut one yourself.) Run the cords through the tube, and allow them to come up through the slit wherever needed. Stick the whole thing behind your desk or nightstand, and you won't have to look at unsightly cords again!

DIY Charging Station Here's an alternative to buying a "charging station" to keep a power strip out of sight: Put the strip in a shoe box, and cut a hole in the back for the power cord to reach the outlet. Cut smaller holes for your charger wires in the lid of the shoe box. Plug the chargers in, thread their wires through the holes, and close the lid.

Upward Spiral When it comes time to throw old school notebooks in the recycling bin, save the spirals—they work great to collect stray cords and wires. If you want, you can even attach the spiral horizontally to a strip of wood using a hot-glue gun. Place it behind your computer and "thread" your cables through the rings. They'll stay separate and it will keep them from falling to the floor when not in use.

lattice that you store the wrapping paper on. Just slide the tubes between the wires and ceiling and they'll be safe, secure, and out of sight.

Gardening Command Center Those hanging vinyl shoe holders can store much more than shoes! Repurpose an old shoe organizer as a storage center for your gardening tools. Just tack it up on the wall in your garage, basement, or shed and you'll have organized storage for all of your small items.

Who Knew? Classic Tip

Looking for a container to store iPod earbud headphones where they won't get tangled? Coil the cord and then place it inside an old cassette case. Your headphones will be safe, and your friends can admire the *Flashdance* sound track decoration on the outside. So retro!

Solve Cord Discord Here's a handy way to mark your electrical cords so you know your printer cord from your lamp cord from your clock cord: Use bread bag tags! Write the appliance name (or first initial) on the tag and clip it to the appropriate cord.

Retrofit a Drawer for Hanging Files No filing cabinet? No problem! You can turn almost any drawer into one suitable for hanging files. All you need is a drawer that is deep enough to hold hanging files, and two tension rods that are usually used for curtains—the smallest and thinnest you can find. Insert the rods in the drawer parallel to each other and perpendicular to the front and back of the drawer. They should be wide enough apart so that the hanging file folders will be able to hang from rods (adjust as necessary). Now you're ready to start filing away!

Kitchen Organizing Ideas

Cut Down on Cabinet Chaos Overcrowded cabinets can be like war zones: You reach to grab something in the back and knock over everything else in your path. That's why we love this easy solution: Turn a baking pan into a "drawer" that you can pull out of your cabinet when you need something. The pan will also catch any spills or leaks, keeping your cabinet cleaner to boot.

Stadium Seating for Jars and Cans When you're searching for something in the pantry, it can be a huge pain to shuffle things around until you find what you're looking for at the very back of the shelf. To simplify the hunt for foods in the pantry, pick up tiered shelf risers at a home goods store. The tiered shelving will place items in the back a few inches higher than those in the front. Everything will be easier to spot—no hassle!

Cookie Cutter Holder Here's another great tip for saving precious space in your kitchen drawers. Keep cookie cutters organized and easy to find by slipping them over a cardboard paper towel tube and standing them upright in the pantry.

Canned Food Storage Canned vegetables can be tricky to store neatly. However, now you can say good-bye to awkward stacks of cans. Grab an upright magazine holder (or pick up a new one), turn it on its back, and lay the cans inside on their sides—the width of the holder is the perfect size for the length of the cans.

Good for Canned Goods The next time you get one of those "fridge packs" of soda, don't throw out the box. You can reuse it to organize your pantry. Fill it with cans of soup, beans, tomatoes, and other canned goods for easy access. It's the perfect design for storage, and luckily it fits cans too!

A Place for Place Mats If you have limited storage space in your kitchen, a binder clip can come in handy for storing placements. Take a binder clip and open the little "wings." Tack one wing against the inside of a kitchen cabinet, or hang it on a nail. Then simply clip to hang your place mats in place!

Who Knew? Classic Tip

Glue one side of a sturdy clothespin to the inside of a cabinet door in your kitchen. They're great for holding plastic shopping bags, and plastic shopping bags are great for holding trash, clean rags, cleaning supplies, and more.

A Hanging System in the Cabinet If your under-the-sink kitchen cabinet is a crowded mess, create a hanger for your spray bottles. Pick up a tension rod at a hardware store, install it inside the cabinet, and hang spray bottles by their handles. Not only will they be easier to grab, you'll also free up valuable storage space.

Add an Extra Lazy Susan If you have a lazy Susan in one of your kitchen cabinets, you know that it makes accessing all of the items in the cabinet so simple. Why not try the same concept elsewhere? Buy another one and use it in the refrigerator to store condiments. Spin it around to grab ketchup, barbecue sauce, mustard, or whatever else is normally at the back of the fridge.

Pantry Pointer When storing foods in opaque containers, such as oatmeal, coffee, flour, and other dry goods, place a rubber band around the outside of the container marking the level of remaining contents. (Then simply move the rubber band down as the level goes down.) It will serve as an easy visual reminder to know when you need to go shopping for that item again.

Double-Decker Utensil Drawers Use your drawer space as efficiently as possible, especially if yours are extra deep. Stack two utensil trays on top of one another, then store your frequently used utensils—forks, spoons, knives, can openers—in the top tray, and those less-often used in the bottom. We keep our chopsticks, skewers, ladles, and garlic press in the bottom tray, and simply lift off the top tray whenever we need them.

Savvy Fridge Storage Juice, soda, beer . . . All those bottles and cans cause mayhem on our refrigerator shelves; they roll around and take up way too much space. Our much-sought-after fix? Stack them on their sides and keep them in place using binder clips! Just affix a clip to a shelf grate and stack the round items against it, using the clip as you would a bookend. The binder clip should hold them in place on one side of the shelf.

Who Knew? Classic Tip

Forget buying one more specialty-organizing device and instead use the time to actually organize. A dish rack or V-rack (meant for roasting) both make great devices for sorting pan lids in the cabinet. Act now and do away with banging and rummaging for good. Simply reach for the lid you need!

Losing Control of Your Cups? Here's a quick and easy way to get more space in your kitchen cupboard without even having to break out a toolbox. Line a metal baking sheet with non-stick shelf liner, then place it on top of four large and sturdy overturned cups. Small glasses will fit underneath it, and you can pile all your plastic cups on top.

Handy Hanging Solution for Foil and Wrap Tired of fishing around in a drawer to find your aluminum foil or plastic wrap? (And if you're anything like us, you use these all the time!) For easier access, try hanging them on a wall or cabinet instead: First, get a package of adhesive-backed plastic hooks from a hardware store. Find an unused spot of wall in your kitchen that would be convenient for grabbing wrap whenever you need it. Stick two hooks to the wall, with enough space between them to fit a box of wrap; then slip the hooks into the sides of the box to hang.

Who Knew? Classic Tip

Here's a great tip if you've ever said, "Where's my ring?" Screw a small hook into the wall near your kitchen sink. It will make a handy place to store your rings while you're doing the dishes.

Hanging Utensil Solution If your cooking utensils are taking up way too much space in the drawer, consider rigging a hanging system: Pick up a stainless steel cabinet handle and some S-shaped hooks from a hardware store. Install the rod across your backsplash or just beneath your cabinets, then hang spatulas, ladles, and whisks on the hooks.

Organize with Vases Put all those vases you get with flower bouquets to good use. Use them on your kitchen counter to store gadgets, large utensils, or anything else that is clogging up your drawers.

Bathroom Storage Solutions

Corralling Toiletries Spice racks can be used beyond the kitchen! Try them in the linen closet to hold makeup bottles, cotton balls, travel-size lotion, and the other nebulous items that collect around your bathroom sink.

Berry Baskets for the Bathroom Why purchase decorative containers for the bathroom when you can reuse pretty fruit baskets for free? Save those colorful plastic berry baskets from your next trip to the grocery store. When you've finished the berries, wash the baskets thoroughly to disinfect, then place them in the bathroom drawers to hold soaps, washcloths, or cotton balls.

Medicine Cabinet Organization If you have a metal medicine cabinet, mount a magnet inside it, and you'll be able to place nail clippers, tweezers, safety pins, or other handy items at your fingertips. And if your cabinet is not made of metal, just glue the magnet inside.

Repurpose a Silverware Tray If your stash of makeup and other beauty products is a disorganized mess, get everything in order with a cutlery tray. Blushes, eye shadows, and nail polishes will fit in smaller compartments while eyeliners, mascaras, and long brushes can be stored in the larger rows.

Shower Rod Hanger Is your shower loaded with loofahs, sponges, and bath toys? Keep them all in one convenient place by installing a spare curtain rod in the back of the shower and hanging them on S-shaped hooks. You can also use the rod to hang-dry bathing suits, wet towels, and clothing, or as hanging storage space for cleaning supplies.

Who Knew? Classic Tip

Many forms of makeup are sensitive to the sun due to their preservatives. Keep your makeup away from the window to ensure it lasts as long as possible.

Save Bathroom Space We love this handy solution for storing brushes, combs, and other hair products: Repurpose soup and other large cans as wall-mounted holders! First, cover the cans with wrapping or contact paper to match your bathroom's design—simply cut the paper to size and glue it around the cans with white craft glue or Mod Podge. Then use adhesive strips (such as the

Command brand) to attach the brush holders to the wall or to the inside of a cabinet door.

Throne Room Reading If you have an extra towel rack in your bathroom that is rarely utilized, use it to neaten up that pile of magazines near the toilet! Open the magazines and drape them on the bar for easy storage that's off the floor.

Jewelry and Other Accessories

Safekeeping for Delicate Jewelry For the safest in safekeeping, pick up a fabric drawer sorter from the local hardware store. Place your favorite and most-often worn items at the front, and your less-frequently-reached-for pieces at the back.

No Time for Lost Earrings Protect your earrings when you're at the gym or the spa by poking them through the holes of your watchband and fastening their backs on the other side. Now you won't have to worry about losing them!

Cork Earring Holder Don't throw away the cork when you finish a bottle of wine. Repurpose it! Cork is a perfect material for storing and toting stud earrings. Cut the cork into thin slices, then poke the earrings through, put the backs back on, and toss them into your toiletry bag when traveling.

Pearl Pointers It's great to organize necklaces by hanging them—all except pearls. These gems are strung on a delicate silk thread that can't sustain the weight. Who knew?

Who Knew? Classic Tip

Need one organized place to store your bracelets? Use a paper towel holder! The standing holders are a perfect place to stack your bangles and other large bracelets—they take up little space and can be found cheaply at discount home goods stores.

Wall-Mounted Jewelry Showcase No more rifling through a cluttered jewelry box to find the pieces you want! Mount decorative knobs or hooks to the wall, then hang necklaces, bracelets, and hair ribbons for an easy-to-access jewelry organizer that doubles as wall décor.

Beautiful Bracelet Stands You could get a pricey jewelry holder to organize your bracelets, but why fork over that cash when you can make your own version that's both elegant and unique? Look around the house for an old, unused candlestick—or visit a thrift shop to find one on the cheap. Give it a nice polish, if needed, then slide your bracelets over the stem and place it on your dresser or vanity.

Who Knew? Classic Tip

You don't have to buy a jewelry organizer to keep your necklaces untangled. Just cut plastic straws in half, thread your necklaces through, and fasten the clasps.

Crafty Craft and Hobby Storage

Sewing Board If you use a sewing machine often, mount a small bulletin board on the wall next to it. Then fill it with pushpins or straight pins. That way when you've got your hands full, you can use the pins to hang extra thread, buttons, bobbins, and other miscellany until you need it.

Junk Drawer Clean-Out Clean out that junk drawer and make sure your pencils, scissors, craft knives, and paintbrushes stay in tip-top shape for longer. Recycle old glass jars from candles or the kitchen to use as protective containers for these tools, which often suffer wear and tear from improper storage. Cut a round piece of felt to fit the inside of a jar, then place it at the very bottom—this will protect the tips of pencils, scissors, and other objects with sharp points.

Label Stored Artwork If you have wall art that isn't yet ready for the wall, take a picture before rolling it into a cardboard tube or covering it in bubble wrap for storage. Tape the photo to the outside of its storage packaging so you'll know in a quick glance what the poster or painting is without having to reopen it.

Make Your Own Memory Boxes You could spend cash on elaborate store-bought boxes to hold old photos, letters, and other special mementos. But why do that when you can use an assortment of boxes you already have? Pretty gift boxes and colorful shoe, hat, and clothing boxes will all do the trick—for free! Label them according to date or special occasion and stick them on a shelf or in a closet for safe storage.

who knew? THE BIG QUESTION

Kids' Artwork

My kids are always coming home from school with art projects. I usually hang them on the fridge for a month or two, but there are too many of them! What do I do when I take them off the fridge? I love them too much to throw them away! **—Caitlyn Fulmer, via Facebook**

Kids' Art Book We get it: Your refrigerator, bulletin board, and various walls around the house are covered in one-of-a-kind kids' artwork, and it's wonderful, but it has to stop. One idea is compiling them into a keepsake binder, using large plastic sleeves to hold bulkier textured work like macaroni, beaded, and sparkle art. Leave the binder on display so guests can view a retrospective of your child's artwork—or store it safely in a box until your little Picasso has more to add.

Storage in an Unexpected Place Store your kids' artwork in a cardboard pizza box! Not only are they sturdy and easy to stack and store, they're also free—the best perk of all. Ask a nearby pizza joint if they can spare any extras that don't have grease stains.

Another Homemade Storage Option The school year is over, and you need a place to store the kids' artwork and other papers. Try rolling them tightly in paper towel tubes so they won't crease, then label the outside, so you know what's what. Paper towel tubes can also be used to store marriage certificates and other important documents.

A Novel Knitter's Trick Knitters rejoice! Here's a super-easy and practical way to organize, store, and work with yarn. Transform old tissue boxes into yarn dispensers! Place one spool in each box, then either poke a small hole through one side and thread the yarn through it, or simply use the opening at the top. You can even secure the boxes together with tape to form one large multicolored yarn dispenser.

Keep Yarn Untangled Here's a crafty idea for keeping your yarn in order: Place one ball of yarn inside a baby wipes container and pull the loose end through the opening at the top. No tangles, no knots!

Who Knew? Classic Tip

You've lost the wick of an old candle, and you were never really crazy about the scent anyway. Turn your old candle into a pincushion by simply sticking pins in the top or the sides. The wax will even help them slide more easily into cloth.

Handle Candles with Care Keep your unused candles intact with this easy storage trick: Cover them in tissue paper and slip them into a cardboard paper towel tube.

If you like, label the tubes by color, scent, and length so you know what to grab first. No more dented, cracked, and crushed candles in your junk drawer!

Portable Beads An old CD jewel case lined with double-sided tape can be used to store beads for arts and crafts projects. This is especially handy if you like to bring supplies with you to beading groups or on vacation.

A Folder Full of Memories If you're at all like us when it comes to digital photos, you have an impossible time keeping your pics organized, not to mention continually saved on a backup drive or disc! (It almost makes us miss when cameras had real film.) While you may not have time to organize and label every photo, here's a simple strategy you can use to at least cut through the chaos and get a handle on your photo collection. Every time you upload photos to your computer, pick a few of your absolute favorites from the event or trip and keep them all in the same folder on your computer. Now, you only have to back up this folder to make sure your most precious moments are saved, and it makes organizing easier: Use separate folders for different children and other family members and friends. When it comes time to gather pictures for a special event like a wedding, you just need to refer to that folder to choose a few of the honoree. Better yet, when your children leave home, you can give them a copy of the folder (in whatever form exists in the future!) and they'll have photos from their entire childhood in one place.

Closet Chaos Solved

Track Your Clothing Habits Many professional organizers agree that we wear 20 percent of our clothes 80 percent of the time. To keep track of your most frequently worn clothing, try this hanger monitoring system: Place all hangers backward on the rod. When you take a piece of clothing out of the closet to wear, turn its hanger in the other direction. Use this system for a few weeks, and you'll have a good idea of which clothes you reach for the most. After a few months, you'll have a good idea of which clothes you need to get rid of.

Virtual Fashion Organizer Never spend another morning agonizing over what to wear! The Stylebook app (StyleBookApp.com) makes organizing your closet and selecting outfits easier than ever. Take photos of your clothing and label each item by color, style, season, or brand; then mix and match pieces to create new outfits anytime you want a fresh look. You can also add items you've found online to your Stylebook closet—that way, you can see how they'll fit with the rest your wardrobe before you make a purchase. And, best of all, Stylebook's calendar allows you to track the dates you've worn an outfit or particular piece of clothing: You'll cut down on repeats and ensure that your style is sharp every day!

Who Knew? Classic Tip

Double the space in your closet without buying one of those expensive "cascading hangers." Instead, offset your hangers with soda can tabs (aka pop tops)! Run the head of a hanger through the top of the tab and hang as you normally would. Then place another hanger in the bottom hole of the tab. Two hangers, and only one spot taken up!

Closet Options If you have one of those plastic six-pack rings used to hold together cans of soda, save it for your closet! It's perfect for organizing scarves, belts, ties, or anything else you can thread through the plastic holes. Just hang one ring from the six-pack plastic over the top of a hanger and use the other five to neatly hang your accessories.

Easily Organize Kids' Clothes Bargains Taking advantage of store sales, yard sale finds, and hand-me-downs can get overwhelming when you try to figure out what size of what you have, especially if you have several kids to clothe. An easy fix is to organize the clothes in plastic bins that you've labeled by size. Just use one bin for each size that your child will grow into soon. That way, if you hit a great end-of-season sale you can stock up on bigger sizes, and when your child grows into the items, they'll be organized and easy to find.

Who Knew? Classic Tip

Don't throw away the little *z*-shaped hooks that come with dress socks—use them as tie holders! Slip them onto a hanger, and they are perfect for hanging a tie that accompanies a particular suit.

Roll 'Em Up Organize your tights and pantyhose in paper towel tubes. Use a marker or felt-tipped pen to label what's inside each one so you don't have to defeat the purpose of streamlining by yanking them all out on the mornings when you're in a rush. (You really can stop the meltdowns with a little planning!) The tubes also protect the tights from getting snagged in the drawer.

Bag Your Purses If you're putting away a purse you don't think you'll use for a few weeks or month, stuff some plastic grocery bags inside. This will ensure the purse keeps its shape—and give you something to do with those bags!

These Boots Are Made for Hangin' Instead of storing boots on the floor, where they bend and wrinkle thanks to that pesky ol' gravity, use pants hangers with clips to hang them in a closet. Not only will they stay straight and like-new for longer, they'll also be organized and out of the way.

Help Boots Keep Their Shapes Another idea for when boot season is over, keep them upright and in good shape by sticking a few paper tower tubes inside before you tuck them away for storage.

Hanging Sandal Storage Need an out-of-the-way spot to stash your flip-flops and sandals? Easily transform a standard wire hanger into a flip-flop hanger, and you'll never be digging at the back of your closet for dusty flip-flops again. First, find some thin wire hangers—they should be easy to bend with your hands. With needle-nose pliers, snip off the bottom rung of the hanger. Now bend the remaining wire ends up to create two U shapes on either side of the hanger. You should be able to easily slip the strap of your flip-flops over the U you just made to hang them in your closet! But before you do, use the pliers to curl the sharp wire ends back toward the wire to protect yourself. Finally, find some space in your closet or install a new rod hanger, and hang your flops!

Who Knew? Classic Tip

Our closets are kind of a mess, but we manage never to misplace part of a sheet set. That's because after washing and folding the pieces, we put the whole set right inside one of the pillowcases, which is a convenient way to make sure everything stays in one place.

The Best Place to Store Soap If you've just purchased a new bar of soap, take it out of its box or wrapper and place it in your linen closet. The exposure to the air will harden the soap slightly, which will help it last longer. Meanwhile, it will freshen your closet while it's waiting to be used in the shower.

Storing Tablecloths Why fold linen tablecloths, which will only mean having to iron them again to get the creases out? Instead, hang them over a curtain rod. It's easy enough to nail a rod inside a closet against the side or back wall. Then you'll always know where to find them, or, better yet, be able to direct someone else their way so that you can attend to whatever's burning in the stove.

Heaven Scent If your wonderfully scented candle is almost completely gone, it's easy to keep the smell with you! Carefully cut or break the remaining candle it into pieces, then put them in an old sock or nylon and hang in your closet. The enclosed space will be filled with your candle's scent every time you open the closet door.

Cleaning Caddy We are always (always!) looking for ways to make household chores easier—and we've found this storage idea to be a nice help. To simplify cleanup time, collect all of your most-used cleaning products into one portable hanging caddy. When you're not cleaning, hang it on the back of a door or store it away in a closet.

Shower Hook Solution Shower hooks use a lot less space than hangers and they're great for keeping large bags from slumping and losing shape on your closet shelves. You can easily store three or so bags with one hook!

chapter 9

Clever Cooking Tips

Saving Time in the Kitchen

Curing Cooking Conundrums

Kitchen Tool Know-How

Better Baking and Desserts

Secrets for Boosting Flavor and Nutrition

Saving Time in the Kitchen

Speed Up a Slow Roast The dinner party guests have eaten their way through the hors d'oeuvres, but the roast you're making still isn't close to being done. Speed up the process by making incisions in the meat every inch or so (don't cut more than halfway down) and then tying the roast together with string. The heat will be better able to penetrate through the incisions, and you'll get dinner on the table sooner.

Neat Tip for Meat Stainless steel rods are often using in construction or crafts. But they can also come in handy in the kitchen! When cooking dense meats such as whole chicken legs, beef, or pork in the oven, insert a clean, stainless steel rod into the meat. It will serve as a heat conductor, allowing the inside of the meat to cook at the same rate as the outside. You'll never again have the problem of a perfectly burnished exterior, while the insides are undercooked and bloody.

Kebab How-to Grilling up kebabs this summer? Make meat removal as easy as possible by spraying skewers with cooking spray before assembling them. The food will slip right off the skewer, no knives necessary! And, more

who knew? THE BIG QUESTION

Saving Time at Your Barbecue

I'm having a big BBQ, and I only have one grill. Are there any tips for saving time without sacrificing taste? **—Christian Midura, via Facebook**

Quick Barbecued Ribs If you're making ribs, here's how to get that lip-smacking, fall-off-the-bone texture without the long cooking time. Put 2 pounds of ribs in a bowl, and coat with a cup of your favorite barbecue sauce. Cover the bowl, and microwave it for eight minutes. Then turn the ribs, and return them to the microwave for another eight to 10 minutes. After you pull them out, grill the ribs over high heat for a few minutes per side until beautifully burnished. Result? Tender, juicy ribs faster than Rachael Ray can say "30 Minute Meals."

Start Burgers in the Oven Burgers, too, can be started before they get to the grill. Put them on a foil-lined baking sheet and bake for five minutes at 400° before throwing on the barbecue.

Slow-Cooker Hot Dogs It may sound surprising, but you can actually cook hot dogs in the slow cooker. If you cook them for four hours on low, they'll taste like they were cooked on a roller grill at the ballpark! Don't add any additional water to the Crock-Pot, as the hot dogs will release water as they cook. If you want to give them a grilled taste, throw them on the grill just long enough for them to get lightly charred.

importantly, no risk of flinging your meat from the skewer to the floor.

Quick Chop Garlic Mince garlic more quickly and efficiently by adding a pinch of salt. The salt helps break down the garlic into a paste and absorbs some of the juices so that the garlic doesn't stick to your knife.

Who Knew? Classic Tip

The best way to thaw turkey is on a shallow baking sheet in the refrigerator, in its original packaging, allowing 24 hours for every five pounds of bird. But if it's Thanksgiving morning and you've forgotten to stick the bird in the fridge, the fastest, safest method of thawing frozen poultry fast is to place it—still wrapped in plastic—in a bowl (or bucket) of cold water. Check the water regularly and change it as the water warms up—you should never use hot water for large pieces of meat, as it will promote bacterial growth.

Food Safety First When you're making hamburgers, place a sheet of plastic wrap down on your platter before adding the raw patties. Once you've added them to the pan or the grill, you can toss the plastic, and the platter underneath will still be clean for the cooked burgers. That way you don't have to wash two dishes, and you protect your family from potentially harmful bacteria.

On a Roll Make bacon slices easier to separate by rolling the package lengthwise and wrapping with a rubber band. Keep it stored that way in the refrigerator and the bacon strips will already be somewhat separated when you reach into the package.

Quick Thickeners An easy method of thickening stews, soups, or creamed vegetables is to add a small amount of quick-cooking oats, a grated potato, or some instant mashed potatoes. Never add flour directly, as it will clump. But if you're a particularly prepared cook, you can combine a stick of melted butter with ½ cup flour, then place it in a covered bowl in the refrigerator and let it harden. Then when you want a thickener, simply add some of this special mixture. It melts easily and will thicken without lumps.

How to "Peel" a Pomegranate Fresh pomegranates are delicious and super-nutritious, but we always thought it was a pain to separate all of the tiny seeds—until we learned this tip: First halve the fruit, and place it in a bowl of cold water. Then scrape the seeds from the pith while it's in the water. They'll be easier to remove, and you won't have to worry about pomegranate juice flying everywhere. Once you've removed the seeds, drain them in a fine mesh strainer. Keep them in a covered container in the refrigerator for easy, healthy snacking.

Who Knew? Classic Tip

For a quick and easy way to pit cherries, use a pastry bag tip. Just set the tip on a cutting board with the jagged edge pointed up, then firmly press the cherry down on top of it. Be careful not to cut your fingers!

Instant Watermelon Sorbet The next time you buy a watermelon, skip the slices and get out the ice-cream scoop. The scoop allows you to dish out the tasty fruit just like you would ice cream or sorbet. Kids will love it served this way, and it's great for dessert!

Secrets to Chopping Dried Fruit If you've ever tried chopping dried fruit, you know it can be a mess because the pieces get stuck to the knife. Make the process easier by sticking the fruit in the freezer for an hour before chopping. You can also try spraying your knife lightly with a cooking spray like Pam.

Corn on the Cob on the Grill Nothing says summer like freshly picked sweet corn. When it's grilled, it takes on a smoky-sweet flavor that's irresistible. Try this simple trick to keep those kernels juicy. First, husk the corn, removing any silk. Then soak the ears in salted water for 10 to 15 minutes. Not only will you season the corn, but the water will help the corn stay moist on the grill.

Corn off the Cob Use a Bundt pan to make it easier to cut fresh corn kernels. Hold the cob over the center hole so that the tip is just touching as you shave off the kernels, which will fall directly into the basin part of the pan.

Who Knew? Classic Tip

Need to quickly peel tomatoes for a recipe? The easiest way is to place them in a pot of boiling water for a minute. The skins will practically fall off.

Slice Onions with Ease As much as we love sliced onions in everything from salads and sandwiches to soups and stews, slicing them is always a messy, stinky chore—and we often end up with chunks rather than thin, delicate slices. To get slim onion slices with less hassle, we've discovered that another standard culinary tool does the job even better than the fanciest of kitchen knives: the potato peeler! Simply shave an onion with the peeler to get restaurant-quality slices.

Easy-Peasy Potato Prep Our family loves our potatoes, whether they're mashed or roasted or boiled or fried. Unfortunately, preparing them is almost always a time-sucking chore. Thanks to this clever tip, however, you can slice up those yummy potatoes in one quick step. Just use an apple slicer! Cut one potato in half and run it through the slicer.

Who Knew? Classic Tip

Did you know that wrapping a potato in foil won't actually make it bake faster? Rubbing it lightly with vegetable oil, however, will.

Easily Separate Tortillas You may have noticed that refrigerated flour tortillas tend to stick together. Get them unstuck in a hurry by wrapping them in a damp paper towel and putting them in the microwave for 15 to 20 seconds. You'll be able to separate them easily without tearing.

Curing Cooking Conundrums

Perfect Hard-Boiled Eggs Have you ever wondered if there's a way to keep the green out of hard-boiled egg yolks? Well, there is! It's as simple as turning the water off as soon as it comes to a boil. Letting the eggs cook in the warm water for 10 minutes will reduce the reaction that causes the green tint.

Who Knew? Classic Tip

Next time you need buttermilk in a recipe, don't go buy a whole carton that you'll later throw away half-full. Instead, make an easy buttermilk substitute by adding a tablespoon of vinegar to a cup of milk and letting it stand for five minutes to thicken.

Shrinkage Stopper Bacon that doesn't shrink means more for your money—and more bacon that you get to put in your dish! Keep bacon from shrinking so much by adding it to a cold pan rather than a hot. Then cook it over medium heat.

Reduce Roast Beef Splatters Roast beef has a tendency to splatter both in the oven and all over the stove when you take it out. Keep the splatters and resulting smoke to a minimum by placing some water in the bottom of the pan before it goes in the oven. Monitor it periodically and add more if needed.

Splatter Shield Keep bacon from splattering all over the stove (and the cook) by adding a few celery leaves to the pan. Who knew?

Who Knew? Classic Tip

There are few kitchen disasters more disheartening than burning a roast. But there's help! If you burn or scorch a roast, remove it from the pan and cover it with a towel dampened with hot water for about five minutes, which will stop the cooking. Then remove or scrape off any burnt areas with a sharp knife, and put the roast back in the oven to reheat if necessary.

Sticky Solution Here's a simple tip: If you wet your hands with cold water before shaping hamburger patties or meatballs, the mixture won't stick to your fingers.

No Wine? No Problem Making a recipe that calls for wine and don't have any on hand (or prefer not to use it)? Try these easy substitutions. Replace red wine with cranberry juice and white wine with white grape or apple juice. Your dish will taste just as good and you saved money too!

Ham Too Salty? A little salt in ham is a good thing, but if your ham slices are too salty, place them in a dish of low-fat milk for 20 minutes before heating, then rinse them off in cold water and dry them with paper towels. The ham won't pick up the taste of the milk, but will taste much less salty.

The Measure of Your Fish It can be tricky to figure out the proper cooking time for fish. If you've ever overcooked an expensive piece of halibut, you know what we mean! To avoid this problem, measure the fish at its thickest part. You can estimate 10 minutes of cooking time for every inch of thickness.

No-Stick Grilled Scallops Grilled scallops can be a special treat, but only if you don't leave half of them stuck to your grill's grate! Try this trick at your next barbecue to ensure great results. Whisk together 3 tablespoons oil, 1 tablespoon all-purpose flour, and 1 teaspoon cornstarch;

who knew? THE BIG QUESTION

Eliminating Fish Smell

I'm trying to lose weight, so I've been making fish for dinner. But my husband won't stop complaining about the smell! Is there anything I can do so that it won't stink up the whole house when I cook fish?

—Ellie von Mehren, via Facebook

Something Smells Fishy! Fresh fish is a great weeknight dinner idea for busy families: It's healthy, delicious, and cooks in just a few minutes. However, the smell that lingers in the pan after it's cooked can be less than desirable. Eliminate it by pouring about a quarter cup of plain white vinegar into the pan after you're done cooking. Let the vinegar simmer and the smell in your kitchen will be gone in five minutes or less!

Get Rid of Fish Odor Before It Starts When frying up fish in a pan, add a dollop of peanut butter. It won't affect the taste of the fish, but it will affect the odor—peanut butter contains a chemical that absorbs that stinky fish odor, so your whole house doesn't have to.

Zap Microwave Odors Fresh fish is a dinnertime treat, but a fresh fish smell in your microwave is not. Get rid fish odor in your microwave by putting a quartered lemon or a small bowl of vanilla in your microwave for a minute or two on high.

brush this mixture all over the scallops before grilling, and they'll brown without sticking.

Knock Out Fishy Smells We know fresh fish should always smell clean like the sea. However, every once in a while, you do end up with fillets that are a bit, well, fishy-smelling. To neutralize this odor, soak the raw fillets in a pan with 2 cups water and 1 tablespoon baking soda. Wait 10 minutes, rinse, and pat dry. The smell will be virtually gone!

Freshen Up Burnt Fish You went a bit overboard with the blackened catfish, and now it's a little too black. Freshen up burnt fish with some chopped parsley. It will help neutralize the burnt flavor and may just save dinner!

Easy-to-Remove Spices If you're cooking with herbs that will need to be removed before eating, make them easy to remove by putting them all in a tea infuser before you add them to your dish.

Save a Salty Dish It's been said that you can always add more salt to a dish, but you can never take it away. While that's true, you can tame down an over-salted dish by adding ¼ teaspoon vinegar and ¼ teaspoon sugar to the food. Mix well, and taste. If it's still too salty, keep adding this combination in small increments until you've balanced out the flavors.

Wiggle It, Just a Little Bit Use a paperclip to pit olives without crushing them! First, unfold a paperclip into the shape of an "S," leaving one small loop. Insert that loop into the top of the olive, and begin to wiggle the pit loose, pulling it out the other side. You'll be left with an intact olive!

Who Knew? Classic Tip

Dried spices can lose their flavor quickly. Luckily, it's easy to perk them back up before using them in your dish. Just toast them in a pan for a minute or two, and their flavors will be revived.

Coconut-Cracking Tip There's nothing better than fresh coconut, and nothing worse than trying to crack it open. Make the process a little easier by sticking the entire coconut in a 350° oven for about 20 minutes. Remove it, and allow it to cool for a few minutes before tapping on it with a hammer until it cracks open.

Lemon Lessons Your recipe calls for 2 tablespoons lemon juice, and you're standing at the store wondering how much juice is in a lemon. Here's a rule of thumb to help: You can generally count on getting 2 to 3 tablespoons juice and 1 tablespoon zest from a lemon.

Who Knew? Classic Tip

If you slice open a mango and it tastes too acidic, place it in warm (not hot) water for 10 minutes. This will speed up the process of its starches turning into sugars, and it will be sweet in no time! Just make sure not to leave it in the water for more than 10 minutes, as it might begin to shrivel.

For Runny Honey Some varieties of honey have a tendency to crystallize. To restore its original liquid texture, place the jar in a bowl of hot water for five to 10 minutes, and then stir.

On the Chopping Block Making a Chinese stir-fry that calls for both ginger and garlic? Chop the ginger last. It will help eliminate the garlicky smell from your hands and the cutting board.

Butter Me Up Butter is delicious to use for sautéing, but it burns quickly. To raise butter's smoke point (the temperature at which it burns), add a little vegetable oil to the pan. Vegetable oil is made for cooking at higher temperatures.

Who Knew? Classic Tip

If you bought a whole bunch of avocados for your guacamole and one or two are still not ripe enough to use, try this tip—which isn't ideal, but will do the trick. Prick the skin of the unripe avocado in several places, then microwave it on high for 40 to 70 seconds, flipping it over halfway through. This won't ripen the avocado, but it will soften it enough that you'll be able to mash it with ripe avocados and your guests won't notice the difference.

The Brown Bag Trick Fruit normally gives off ethylene gas, which hastens ripening. Some fruits give off more gas than others and ripen faster. Other fruits are picked before they are ripe and need a bit of help. If an unripe fruit is placed in a brown paper bag, the ethylene gas it gives off does not dissipate into the air but is trapped and concentrated, causing the fruit to ripen faster. To get it to ripen even more quickly, add a ripe apple—one of those ethylene-rich fruits.

A Sweeter Banana Saver You're hosting brunch and slicing up bananas for a platter of fresh fruit. To keep the bananas from browning before your guests arrive, toss them with a little orange or pineapple juice. The flavor is not as sour as lemon juice (which many cooks use), and it works just as well.

A Banana Myth Busted If your bananas ripen before you have a chance to eat them all, don't toss them—put them in the fridge! You may have been told never to put bananas in the refrigerator, but if you seal them tightly in a Ziploc bag (squeezing out as much air as possible), you'll slow down the ripening process and be able to keep them fresh for a few more days.

Cut Down on Cabbage Odor Whether you're braising or boiling cabbage, you know that it has a tendency to get a bit odoiferous. To reduce those unpleasant sulfur aromas, try one of these tips: Add a bit of celery to the cooking pot, toss in a whole walnut in its shell, or add half a lemon to the pot.

Crisp Up Your Veggies Limp carrots putting a crimp in your crudité tray? Get the crunch back by soaking them in a bowl of ice water for 20 minutes. They'll be as good as new! You can also try this trick with lettuce and herbs like cilantro.

Who Knew? Classic Tip

If you burned the rice, fear not! It's white bread to the rescue. Get rid of the scorched taste by placing a slice of fresh white bread on top of the rice while it's still hot, and covering it for a few minutes.

Stop Bean Boil-Over Never have the water from your beans simmer onto the stove again! If you add a table-spoon of oil to a pot of boiling beans, you'll help prevent the pot from boiling over. (This tip is a must if you use a pressure cooker!)

Unstick Your Rice If your pasta or rice sticks together when you cook it, next time add a teaspoon of lemon juice to the water when boiling. Your sticky problem will be gone! The lemon juice will also help naturally fluff up the rice.

Pasta Water Pass Your recipe calls for a cup of water left over from the pot of pasta, but you accidentally poured it all into the sink when you were draining the noodles. Luckily, there's an easy substitute: mix 1 cup water with ¼ teaspoon cornstarch and microwave until warm.

A Bright Idea You may have noticed that when you boil sweet potatoes, some of their vibrant orange color fades. To keep them looking bright, add the juice of half a lemon to the boiling water. The citric acid will preserve the color.

Who Knew? Classic Tip

Cooking Thanksgiving dinner and your vegetables turned to mush? Simply add some herbs along with tomato sauce or cream. Then top with cheese and/or breadcrumbs and stick in the oven for 30 minutes. Your family is sure to be impressed with your new recipe for "vegetables gratin"!

Cola for Beans We all know about the—ahem—side effects that beans can have on some people. To help prevent gas before it starts, add a half a can of cola to the water while you're cooking the beans. Surprisingly, the carbonated soft drink prevents the undesired aftereffects.

No More Smushy Sandwiches! We love this idea for keeping bagels intact when packed into lunchboxes. If you have old CD spindles that are no longer used on account of an MP3 upgrade, use them to store your bagel sandwiches! The spindle fits right through the center hole of your bagel, and the hard plastic covering will protect it from getting smashed inside a packed lunch.

Smart Taco Tip Yay for taco night . . . until the taco shells crumble. Stop taco shell cracks before they start by lining each one with a lettuce leaf. The lettuce will keep moist ingredients from weakening the shell, making sure your toppings stay put.

Kitchen Tool Know-How

Genius Bottle-Top Trick When you've used all the ketchup in a plastic squeeze bottle, throw the cap in the dishwasher to remove the caked-on ketchup. Keep it, along with other condiment bottle tops, handy in the kitchen. When your current bottle top gets all mucked-up, simply switch it out with a clean top and throw the dirty one in the dishwasher.

Fun with Funnels Your favorite angel food cake recipe calls for a dozen egg whites, but you can never get the hang of separating eggs properly. Try a funnel! Place a narrow funnel over your bowl and crack the egg into the funnel. The white will filter through to the bottom, and (as long as it's not broken) the yolk will stay behind.

Who Knew? Classic Tip

If your knife is rusty, it's time to chop some onions. Believe or not, onions will remove rust from metal objects. Plunge the knife into the biggest onion you can find, let it sit for a few seconds, then pull it out. Repeat this process until the rust has dissolved, then wash as usual and dry.

Like-New Knives Most knife sharpeners are ceramic, which means it's relatively easy to find a stand-in if your knife is dull and you don't have a sharpener at home. Get an old ceramic flowerpot or mug and turn it upside down. Then run your knife at a 20° angle back and forth across the edge five to 10 times.

An Unconventional Cake-Cutter Need a slicing dynamo in the kitchen? Don't fork over tons of cash for a fancy new utensil—head to the home-repair aisle instead! There, you'll find drywall mud knives that will do an even better job with cakes, tarts, and dessert bars than a regular old kitchen knife. Bonus: Most cost around $10!

Slice Without Sliding Felt is useful for more than just kids' craft projects. Cut out four little squares and place them underneath your cutting board for slip-free slicing.

Who Knew? Classic Tip

Want to make perfect slow cooker creations every time? The secret is steam. Make sure to cover the food with enough liquid to generate sufficient steam. When possible, cook on the highest setting for the first hour, then reduce it to low if necessary.

Nonstick Pan Preserver There's food stuck to your (supposedly) nonstick pans. You want to scrape it off, but are afraid of harming the finish. Our solution? A plastic lid from a take-out or other container. Push it against the pan and gently rub it on the spot to scrape without scratching.

Listen to Your Double Boiler You know you shouldn't walk away from a double boiler, but inevitably the sound of your kids fighting, your cat scratching the sofa, or something else calls you away for a moment. Here's some extra protection to make sure your delicate foods don't get scorched: Add a few marbles to the bottom of the pan. If you hear them start to bounce around, you'll know the water level is too low.

A Cup for Your Kids Make your own version of nonslip kids' cups using mugs or cups you already have. If your cups are slippery, put a wide rubber band around them so children can get a better grip.

Grownup Use for a Sippy Cup It's a beautiful, fresh, colorful salad until—no! Close the floodgates! It's over-dressed and barely edible. Next time, save your salad with a baby sippy cup. Mix your vinaigrette inside the cup, shake, and scatter it over the salad with its perfectly sized spout.

Crush Garlic Without a Press Using garlic but short a garlic press? This kitchen trick gets the job done so well, you may not ever have to buy a press again. Use a regular old fork as you would use a grater: Hold it so the tines are pressed against your work surface, then rub a peeled garlic clove across the tines to "crush" it into a paste. This will take some forceful action in your rubbing motion, but you'll get perfectly crushed garlic for your dish.

Kitchen Spoon Saver Keep your wooden spoon from falling into your saucepot forever with a clothespin. Simply clip the clothespin on the edge of your pot, and it will provide a convenient rest to lay your spoon against!

An Exhausting Suggestion If you're going to be frying or preparing a dish that produces a lot of smoke, cook it on the back burner! In most kitchens, the exhaust fans are not centered over the stove but instead are placed closer to the back, so if you cook on the back burners, you'll remove twice as much smoke.

See Also . . . Learn how to make some kitchen utensils yourself in the Easy DIYs chapter.

Better Baking and Desserts

Stop Squashing Your Bread You just brought home a beautiful loaf of freshly baked bread from the market. Avoid squashing it when slicing it by flipping it over and cutting through the soft bottom first. Your knife will move through it smoothly, and you'll be able to cut the crusty top without flattening the whole loaf.

Who Knew? Classic Tip

Bread gone stale? Simply wet your fingers and flick some water on the top and sides of the loaf. Then wrap in foil and heat in a preheated 250° oven for 10 minutes. It will taste fresh again!

Butter Bread Better Have you ever tried buttering a piece of bread only to end up tearing holes into it? Try buttering before you slice it off of the loaf. That way, you'll have a firmer base and will be less likely to tear the tender crumb.

Supersoft Biscuits For supersoft biscuits, brush them with milk or melted unsalted butter before baking, then arrange them in a cake pan so the sides touch one another.

Dust Your Nuts Nuts and dried fruit are the perfect addition to muffins, breads, and other baked goods. But sometimes, after you pour the batter into the pan, they sink to the bottom. To keep this from happening, dredge the mix-ins in flour before stirring them into the batter. That way, they'll stay suspended in the cake and won't all end up at the bottom of the finished product.

Easy Walnut Cracking Need to crack a lot of walnuts? Soak them overnight in salted water and they'll open more easily.

De-Salt Your Nuts Your recipe for peanut butter cookies calls for unsalted nuts, but you only have a can of the salted variety. Make them unsalted by placing them in boiling water for a minute or two, then draining. To eliminate any remaining moisture, spread the nuts on a cookie sheet and bake in a 225° oven until they're dry, about five minutes. Cool, and then use your newly unsalted nuts in your recipe.

Better with Buttermilk To give your muffins an extra tang and an incredibly light texture, swap out the milk for buttermilk. In addition, for every cup of milk that you substitute, add ½ teaspoon baking soda to the batter. You can also try this tip with plain yogurt. You'll win raves for that extra-special something in your muffins!

Mind Your Muffins Do your muffins have soggy bottoms? The fix is easy. Just wait 10 minutes after you take them out of the oven, then transfer them to a wire rack where they can finish cooling.

Who Knew? Classic Tip

Making cupcakes or muffins but don't have enough batter to fill the entire tin? Before sticking the pan in the oven, fill the empty cups halfway with water. This will extend the life of the tin and ensure the muffins bake evenly.

For Stuck Muffins If you appreciate second uses for household items as much was we do, you'll love this tip. If you're having trouble getting your muffins out of the pan, try using a (clean) shoehorn! The curved shape should help them pop right out.

Baking Basic Did you know that it takes most ovens up to 15 minutes to pre-heat? For the best results when baking, always make sure you've given your oven enough time to pre-heat. If it's not quite hot enough, it can make a big difference with your recipe.

Batter Up For best results when baking cakes or cupcakes, there are two rules we always follow: Use a cool pan, and never fill the tin more than 2/3 full. We can't guarantee other mistakes won't happen, but at least we've got the basics covered!

Who Knew? Classic Tip

The bad news is that your cake is stuck to the pan. The good news is that it's easy to get it out intact—you just need to heat up the bottom of the pan by submerging it in hot water. Once the pan heats back up, use a knife to easily dislodge your still-perfect cake.

Rescue a Layer Cake You decided to attempt a three-layer cake, and can't believe how great it looks. The problem? The layers are sliding so much it's starting to look like a Jenga game waiting to topple. Fix by cutting two straws so they're just shorter than the height of the cake, then insert and frost right over them (use four straws if it's really shaky). If anyone notices your cheat, they'll just be impressed!

Maximize Every Morsel Got a round cake to serve for dessert? Rather than cutting long messy slices, try this

THE BIG QUESTION who knew?

Icing Cakes

I feel like I'm OK at making cakes, but once it comes to icing them I fall apart. How do I get the icing to look good?

—Lisa, via WhoKnewTips.com

Yes, Really—a Hair Dryer! Making a birthday cake at home is a great way to save at the bakery, but if you're not a cake-decorating genius, it never looks as good as store-bought. To give the icing on top of your cake the silky look of a professionally made one, ice it as usual and then blow a hair dryer over the top for a minute. It will melt the icing slightly, giving it the shiny appearance you're looking for.

Crumb-Free Cake Frosting One of the hardest things about frosting a cake is making sure that crumbs don't turn your smooth icing into a lump-filled mishap. The secret that many pastry chefs use is to dollop spoonfuls of icing a couple of inches apart all over the top of the cake, and then use a spatula to simply spread them out.

Baking Soda to the Rescue Prevent flaking and cracking when making cake frosting by adding a pinch of baking soda when mixing it together.

carving technique to get the most out of your star attraction: Cut a ring around the cake to create a smaller cake at the center. Slice the outer ring into rectangular wedges, and serve these icing-heavy pieces to the kids. Then slice the inner circle as you normally would (into wedges like a pizza); serves these daintier slices to the grown-ups.

Scoop Dreams For perfectly baked cupcakes that are uniform in size, use an ice-cream scoop instead of pouring batter or using a regular spoon.

Who Knew? Classic Tip

If you find that the contents of your brown sugar box have become one giant lump, wrap the box in a ball of foil and bake in a 350° oven for five minutes. It will be back to its old self in no time.

Smooth Cheesecake Finish Ever wondered if there is an easy solution to keep your homemade cheesecake from cracking? There is! As soon as it comes out of the oven, run a knife around the outside edge of the cheesecake to release it from the sides of the pan. That way, as it cools down and contracts it won't get any growing pains.

Stick with the Stick When baking cookies or other desserts, avoid reduced-fat butters or margarines unless the recipe specifically calls for them. These low-fat products have a higher water content than regular butter or margarine, and the finished product will not turn out properly. Use the stick variety of butter or margarine instead.

The Big Chill For better cookies, refrigerate your dough for 30 minutes after mixing it. Not only will the dough be easier to work with, but the cookies will also spread more evenly in the oven.

Who Knew? Classic Tip

Are your cookies stuck to the baking sheet? Work some dental floss between each cookie and the sheet, and you should be able to remove them easily.

Double-Decker If you don't have an insulated or a thick baking sheet and your cookies keep burning, here's a simple solution: Try baking the cookies on two sheets stacked one on top of the other. This will eliminate burned bottoms caused by a too-thin pan.

Fix a Cookie Conundrum Don't let the finishing touch on your peanut butter cookies—flattening the dough with a fork—ruin their appearance! Use a plastic fork rather than a metal one and the dough won't stick to it.

Chopping Chocolate? Chopping chocolate for a sweet recipe can be a real pain, thanks to the tiny shards of chocolate left on your cutting board. Make your job much easier by simply heating the chocolate before you cut it. (One minute in the microwave usually does the trick; heat until the edges start to melt.) The slightly softened chocolate won't splinter as much, making sure you waste very little!

Make Your Own Chocolate Molds If you thought nothing was more fun that chocolate, you haven't tried making chocolate in the shape of your child's favorite plastic toy! And it's easier than you think—the secret is brown sugar. In addition to plenty of brown sugar, you'll need a baking dish, ideally an 8 x 8 square pan. First, fill the pan with tightly packed brown sugar. Next, find a sturdy object you'd like to replicate in chocolate (your child's toy box is often a good place to find something—a plastic bunny would be a good choice at Easter, for example). Press the (clean!) item firmly into the brown sugar so that it leaves an impression and remove. The brown sugar will hold the shape of the object, and you can now use it as a chocolate mold! Simply pour melted chocolate into the mold you've just created, then refrigerate for about 30 minutes, or until hardened. You can then remove your chocolate creation and wow your family!

Secrets for Boosting Flavor and Nutrition

Perfect Poaching Poached eggs are a terrific treat for weekend brunch, but it can be tricky to get the raw eggs into the pan without breaking the yolk. Try using a coffee mug next time. That way, you can partially submerge the mug in the simmering water, giving the eggs a smooth transition to the pan.

Save Your Rinds The rinds of hard cheeses like Parmesan are great flavor enhancers for soups. Add a 3-inch square to your next pot of soup, and when you're serving the soup, break up the delicious, softened rind and include a little of it in each bowl. It's completely edible.

For Cheese Plate Praise Serving cheese and crackers? Always bring cheese to room temperature for one hour before serving it. Even if the cheese melts a little, the flavor will be much better.

Who Knew? Classic Tip

Who doesn't enjoy an iced coffee on a sultry summer day? To make sure melting ice doesn't dilute your drink, make ice cubes using the small amount of coffee left at the bottom of your coffee pot each morning. Use them in your iced coffee and it will never taste watered down. This is also a great tip for iced tea!

Awaken Your Herbs To get the most impact out of your herbs and spices, whether dried or fresh, rub them between your hands before you add them to a dish. You'll release more of the herb's natural flavor, making for a tastier meal.

A Shocking Burger Tip Keep your hamburgers from breaking apart on the grill by sticking them in the freezer for five minutes before cooking. The brief shock of cold will help them keep their shape.

Rinse Away the Fat! For extra-lean ground beef, place the cooked meat in a fine mesh strainer and rinse with hot water. You'll eliminate up to half of the fat content!

Who Knew? Classic Tip

Allowing air to circulate around roasts ensures even, quicker cooking. Elevate the meat by cooking it atop celery ribs, carrot sticks, or thick onion slices. Raising the roast helps get the hot air underneath the meat, and gives it a great flavor!

Sear Skin-Side Down Always cook fish skin-side down first. Not only will it produce a crisp exterior, but you'll also avoid overcooking. A good rule of thumb is to leave the fish skin-side down for ¾ of the cooking time, and only flip it over for a few minutes to finish.

A Must for Fried Chicken Make your fried chicken extra-crispy by adding 3 to 4 teaspoons cornstarch to each cup of flour, or add 1 teaspoon baking soda to the batter. Then sit back and wait for your fried chicken to win raves!

Crispy Chicken Secret We've got the secret to crispy chicken skin: salt! The next time you buy a whole chicken, sprinkle it with about a tablespoon of coarse salt and place it uncovered in the refrigerator overnight. The salt and the dry air in the refrigerator will draw out moisture—the enemy of crispiness—and you'll roast up a super-tasty bird.

Juicy Juice Double the amount of juice you get from a lime or lemon simply by putting it in the microwave for 10 to 15 seconds before juicing it. The heat will soften up the flesh, allowing you to extract every last drop of juice. It's an easy way to get more for your money!

Who Knew? Classic Tip

If your apples are dry or bland, slice them and put them in a dish, and then pour cold apple juice over them and refrigerate for 30 minutes. OK, so it's kind of a cheat, but it will ensure picky eaters get their nutrients!

A Pineapple Pointer Did you know that the natural sugars in pineapple have a tendency to settle on the bottom of the fruit? Get them going in the other direction! Slice off the leaves and turn the fruit upside down on the counter for an hour before slicing. That way, the sugars will be evenly distributed throughout the entire pineapple.

A Wash for Fresh Fruits and Veggies Store-bought produce is often coated with a thin layer of wax applied by distributors to keep it from drying out while shipping. While the wax is FDA-approved, many people would rather not consume it along with their daily dose of fruits and veggies. To remove the wax and all the chemicals and pesticides on the skin of fruits and vegetables, create a baking-soda bath in your kitchen sink by filling it with water and adding about ½ cup baking soda and mixing until it dissolves. Let your produce soak in the bath for a few minutes before removing and drying with a clean towel.

For Spinach, Stick with Stainless Steel If you're making cooked spinach, be sure to use a stainless steel pot or pan. Aluminum will turn the leaves a dark color and give the spinach a metallic taste. If possible, you should also use a stainless-steel knife to chop it. Carbon-steel knives will cause discoloration.

Hold the Salt If your recipe calls for caramelized onions or other vegetables, here's a tip you should know: Don't add salt until the end of the cooking process. Salt draws out moisture, so if you salt at the beginning, the vegetables will steam and you won't get that nice sear you're looking for.

For Whiter Whites When boiling cauliflower, add a tablespoon of vinegar or lemon juice to the water to preserve the white color.

Who Knew? Classic Tip

If your kids don't like vegetables, you'll love this clever way of getting more nutrients into them. If you have too many vegetables to use before they go bad, puree them in a blender with a little bit of lemon juice, then freeze. Defrost and add to sauces, soups, stews, enchiladas, and more—your kids won't be able to taste the difference! The key is to make sure you don't dramatically alter the color of the dish you're serving. So if you're making a white sauce, for instance, try a puree of cauliflower and summer squash. Tomato-based sauces can usually handle one part "green puree" for every four parts tomato sauce. So grind up that broccoli and spinach and get going!

Calcium Counts Sneak some calcium into your kids' food by adding powdered milk to their meals. It'll be inconspicuous to them in dishes such as mashed potatoes, meatballs, and peanut butter sandwiches (mixed in with the peanut butter).

Long Live Lettuce When you bring lettuce home from the supermarket, take it out of the plastic bag it came in and store it in a paper bag. That way, excess moisture will be able to evaporate, and it will last longer.

String Theory Celery strings are hard for our bodies to digest, and can be annoying when you're trying to bite through them. Make your celery easier to eat by removing the strings first. Before you use celery in a recipe, just peel the stringy side of the stalks with a vegetable peeler. It may seem fussy, but it's quick and easy—and you'll never go back once you try it.

Warm as a Cucumber? You may have heard the expression "cool as a cucumber," but did you know that cucumbers should be stored in the warmest part of the refrigerator? If they get too cold, they can get mushy, but if they stay at room temperature, they will go bad quickly. Keep them in the warmest part of your fridge (which is often the vegetable drawer) for best results.

For Better Beans When you're boiling dry beans, hold the salt. If you add salt too soon in the cooking process, the beans can cook unevenly. Wait to add it until the last 30 minutes of cooking. Good to know!

A Nutritional Powerhouse Brown rice is always a healthy choice, but did you know you can make it even healthier? If you allow it to soak for few hours before cooking, it will start to germinate, dramatically increasing the vitamin, mineral, and antioxidant concentration in the rice.

Who Knew? Classic Tip

When storing a cooked roast in the fridge, place it back into its own juices whenever possible. When reheating sliced meat, place it in a casserole dish with lettuce leaves between each of the slices. The lettuce provides just the right amount of moisture to keep the slices from drying out.

Chef's Pasta Trick Before you drain pasta, scoop out a cup of the cooking water. When you toss the pasta with the sauce, add a little bit of the water. The starchy water will help the sauce to cling to the pasta, making for a tastier dish.

Tastier Leftovers When warming leftover baked goods like biscuits and muffins in the microwave, place a mug of hot water in the oven as well. It will help keep the food from drying out, and it will reheat faster.

Soften Hardened Marshmallows If you find an old bag of hardened marshmallows, add a slice of very fresh white bread or half an apple to the bag to soften them. Note that this is not a quick fix: You might need to leave the bag for one or two days until the marshmallows absorb the moisture. But at least you won't have to throw them out!

Fix Lumpy Brown Sugar If you find that the contents of your brown sugar box have become one giant lump, wrap a chunk in a ball of foil and bake in a 350° oven for ten minutes, and it's good to use again. Only bake as much sugar as you need for the recipe, because the heat can change the consistency of the sugar.

Whip It Good Whipping up some cream? Heavy cream will set up faster if you add seven drops of lemon juice to each pint of cream. But you don't necessarily need heavy cream (and all of its calories) if you're making whipped cream. Light cream can be whipped to a firm, mousse-like consistency if you add 1 tablespoon unflavored gelatin dissolved in 1 tablespoon hot water for every 2 cups of cream. After whipping, refrigerate for two hours.

chapter 10

Easy DIYs

DIY Household Objects

Super Bands When you're ready to throw them out, cut rubber gloves into strips with an extra sharp scissors to make rubber bands! The fingers will provide you with small bands and the palm section will give you giant rubber bands with tons of household uses. We find them handy for kindling wood and keeping sports equipment together.

DIY Notepads If you use a lot of notepads around your house like us (we scribble down everything from shopping lists to schedule reminders and, of course, new tip ideas), you can make your own for much less than you'd spend at the store with something called padding compound. Padding compound is a brush-on glue specially designed for binding papers that you can find online or in hobby and craft stores for $10 to $15. Once you have your bottle, you can make hundreds of pads of paper with any scrap paper! All you need is a stack of paper in any size, color, and pattern you like; a piece of same-sized cardboard for backing (optional); a couple of binder clips; a small paintbrush; and the padding compound. First, make sure your stack of paper is flush on one side—to do this, just tap it against a flat surface. If you want a sturdy back for your pad, cut a piece of cardboard to the same size as your notepaper, and place it at the back. Hold the paper stack together with binder clips, one on each side. Using the paintbrush, spread a good amount of padding compound onto the flush end of your stack; you can apply more for extra sturdiness. Let dry, them remove the binder clips. Use decorative paper for a personalized and inexpensive gift!

Who Knew? Classic Tip

Cereal boxes make great stacking trays for your home office. Carefully cut off the top and back of the box, and you have an inbox waiting to happen. If you don't like the Total, Wheaties, and Chex look, spray the boxes with silver spray paint and let dry before using.

New Use for an Old Crib We often run out of space when hanging clothes to dry—so sometimes we have to get crafty! If you have an unused crib in your home, dismantle it and use the sides as drying racks for non-dryer garments. You can mount it to your wall, hang it from the ceiling, or build an easel setup so it sits securely on the ground.

Make Your Own Phone Stand Like most of us, you probably have lots of technological remnants from the '80s. What can you do with old tape cassette cases? Repurpose them for your digital-era gadgets! Open the cassette case all the way, until it's literally inside out, and set it standing on the inside of the back of the case. The front of the case should stick straight up, with a pocket that's perfectly suited to hold a smartphone or other palm-size gadget. Decorate your gadget stand as you like: Line it with decorative paper or draw on it with marker.

Candy Tin Fridge Magnets Do you have any pretty, vintage-looking candy, tea, or spice tins in your cabinets? Once you've used up the ingredients, repurpose the tins as stylish magnets for the refrigerator. Just position a magnet on the inside back wall of the tin, and stick it to your fridge. Or, if the container isn't metal, pick up adhesive magnets from your local hardware store and stick one to the back of each tin.

Shaken, Not Stirred Who needs a martini shaker? Instead of buying this expensive bar tool, simply use a stainless steel thermos with a screw-in lid. If there's no way to close the sipping hole on the top, cover it with your thumb while you shake!

Restaurant-Style Burger Patties Ever notice the perfectly round hamburger patties sold at the supermarket? Your homemade burgers can look restaurant-ready too, no fancy "hamburger press" necessary! Just use the lid from a jar as a mold for your ground beef—large lids for Whopper-size burgers and small lids for sliders. Find a lid that's a bit larger than your buns, cover the underside in a stretch of plastic wrap, and fill it with beef. The plastic wrap makes patty-removal super-easy, and you'll have a flawless and completely uniform batch of burgers in no time!

Who Knew? Classic Tip

You've seen those nifty, colorful jar openers in cool housewares shops, but you might not realize you've got a bunch of tools that are just as effective lying around your garage or basement. Using an X-Acto knife, slice open an old tennis ball and you've got two handy openers—game, set, match. Now pass the olives.

Who Needs a Juicer? Instead of purchasing a handheld juicer (also known as a reamer) for fruit, simply use one blade from a hand mixer instead. Halve the fruit and twist the blade into it for easy juicing.

Make Your Own Bowl Scraper Have you ever seen those bowl scrapers in kitchen stores that sell for $3 to $10? These circular, plastic tools are easy to make at home.

Simply take the lid of a round take-out container, cut it in half, then remove the rim. Instant savings!

Shabby Chic Trivets Hardware and home-improvement stores have lots of ceramic tiles that can be adapted as mix 'n' match trivets. Choose from a variety of designs and colors to add unique accents to your table setting. Protect tables and other surfaces by affixing felt corners (peel and stick) underneath each tile.

No-Cost No-Slip Hangers The hangers in our closet really needed an overhaul: We were tired of finding clothes on the floor, and also not so keen on the prospect of buying all new padded hangers. So we decided to make our own: All you need is a hot-glue gun! Dab glue onto the shoulders or bottom rung of the hangers. Let it dry, then remove any flyaways around the spots of glue. Once the hangers are completely cool, hang your clothes and voila! Shirts, dresses, and pants stay put.

Double-Duty Pincushion If your pins and needles seem dull from use, revamp a pincushion into a handy needle sharpener—all you need is a pad of fine-grade steel wool. Grab enough wool to fit your pincushion, then open the cushion, tightly stuff the new filling inside, and stitch it back up. Every time you poke a needle through the steel wool, you're giving it a good sharpening! While this is not a pincushion for storing your needles (the steel can promote rusting), it's an excellent tool to use while you sew. For storage, keep your pins and needles in a regular pincushion.

Ring Around the Egg Don't buy a specialty gadget to make perfect circles out of poached eggs—just reuse an old tuna can as an egg ring! Remove both ends of the can, and wash it very well in warm, sudsy water. Then place some water in a pan. When it starts to simmer, place the can in, and crack an egg into it for perfect poaching.

Easily Toast Nuts Toasting nuts for a recipe? You can make sure your nuts won't burn, even if you aren't looking at them, by toasting them in a popcorn air popper! Just add ¼ cup nuts, plug in the popper for 60 seconds, and your nuts will be a perfect golden brown.

DIY Wine Rack Here's an adventurous DIY project for a wine lover. Collect 10 to 12 large cans (the kind used for whole peeled tomatoes or the larger size of canned beans). Pull off the labels, clean and dry the cans, remove the tops and bottoms and make sure the edges are smooth. You want to build a sculpture for the wine rack—think of a human pyramid—using a strong glue to bind the cans to-

who knew? THE BIG QUESTION

Homemade Air Fresheners

Is it true you can just make your own air fresheners at home? **—Natalie West, via Facebook**

DIY Freshness It's easy to make your own gel air fresheners at home with this simple recipe: Boil a cup of water, then mix in 1 packet gelatin, 1 tablespoon salt, 15 drops of your favorite essential oil, and several drops of food coloring. Once the gelatin dissolves, pour into a glass cup or jar to set. Keep away from kids and pets and enjoy the scent for a month or more!

Very Vanilla If you love the aroma of vanilla, make an air freshener using vanilla's enticing scent. Just take a small jar and place several cotton balls inside. Squeeze a few drops of vanilla extract onto the cotton balls. Before putting the cover on the jar, use a nail to puncture a few holes into it and *voilà*! You've got your very own vanilla air freshener!

DIY Reed Diffuser You can also make your own reed diffuser. Find a small vase or container you like and buy a packet of diffuser reeds—sold as "refills." First, pour a quarter-cup of mineral oil into a small bowl. Next add a couple tablespoons of vodka and mix well. Then add about 10 drops of your favorite essential oil and stir thoroughly. Finally, pour the mixture into the vase and put in five or six reeds. After a few hours, flip the reeds over and flip them again every few days.

gether. For the balance-challenged, stick with rows of four, four, and two. Others can try alternating two and three, even beginning with the smaller number. You can also make a triangle with each row one can shorter than the row below. For extra pizzazz, spray paint the cans before you start building.

Don't Buy Air Freshener Refills Do you have a plug-in air freshener? You may be able to refill it without buying costly refills that contain toxic chemicals. Instead, use essential oil, which comes in a variety of scents and can be found online or in health-food stores. Remove the wick from the bulb, fill with half water and half essential oil, give it a shake, and put the wick back in. Then plug in for a pleasing scent!

DIY Discs for Candle Warmers If you're a candle lover, you've probably also gotten hooked on candle warmers—electronic warmers that have wax discs that melt and produce a wonderful scent. If you've ever wondered if you could somehow turn old, used-up candles into wax discs, the answer is yes! Here's how: First, scrape out the old wax and place in a double boiler. If you have several candles with different scents, consider combining them by category: For example, pair fall scents like cinnamon and pumpkin, or florals like freesia, sweet pea, and lavender.

Heat in the double boiler until completely melted, then carefully pour into an ice cube tray. Stick the tray in the freezer until the wax hardens again, about 20 minutes, then turn it over to pop out the reshaped candle discs! You should be able to scrape any remaining wax out of the broiler after it hardens again, but if you plan on making wax discs a lot you may want to keep your eyes peeled at thrift shops and garage sales for an old double boiler you can use just for wax.

DIY Resealable Bags If your plastic bags are not resealable, you can seal them yourself with this quick trick: Fold a small piece of aluminum foil over the end you'd like to seal, and iron it so both ends of the foil close over the plastic. This will ensure that the plastic doesn't melt.

The Coolest Cooler You can buy a floating beverage cooler that looks like a pool toy, but why not make your own poolside cooler using a toy wagon, inflatable pool, or small plastic pool? They all make attractive coolers for summertime parties. Fill with ice and drinks and even some pool toys or rubber ducks for a whimsical decorative element.

Modern Light Reflectors You don't need to purchase light reflectors for your driveway if you have CDs or DVDs lying around that don't work or you don't need. Hang them up on the trees and fence posts lining your driveway making sure the shiny side is facing out to catch the car lights. In the daytime they'll glint in the sunlight, appearing to be some sort of modern outdoor sculpture that is sure to impress your guests.

See Also . . . For DIY household cleaners, see the Cleaning Made Easy chapter.

Make Your Own Kids' Toys

Choo-Choo Shoe Box If you have a collection of shoeboxes you don't need, punch holes in the front and back and string them together to make a train. The easiest way is to use one continuous piece of string and simply thread it into and out of each box in a row. If you want to keep the boxes in place you can tie knots bigger than the holes in front and behind each box. It's simple enough to convert the no-nonsense locomotive to a toy train. Simply take the tops off and fill it with small toys.

Ramp It Up Use a poster mailing tube as a ramp for toy cars. Hold it level while your child slides a car in, then raise the end you're holding so the car whizzes down and out the other side. You can also use multiple cars and collect them at one end in a bucket or pan for a pleasing clacking sound as they zip out of the tube and join the heap. When they're all in a pile, dump them out and start again.

Who Knew? Classic Tip

If you have young boys, you'll love this new use for old jeans: Cut off the legs and trim into strips about 2 inches wide and as long as the pants' entire leg. Turn them over so the inner, grayish side is face-up. Then draw dotted yellow lines on them in paint, marker, or even crayon to make fabric streets! Your kid will love driving his toy cars on them.

Paper Log Cabins If you collect enough paper towel tubes you can make your own jumbo "Lincoln Logs." Separate half the tubes and cut out 1½-inch squares at either end. Take the uncut rolls and stack them perpendicularly by sliding the end into the openings you cut.

Colossal Blocks Make towers you can tumble without upsetting your downstairs neighbors! Cereal boxes can easily be converted into oversize blocks for undersize humans. Make sure to shake out any excess Raisin Bran and then tape the top shut with packing tape. Add shoeboxes to the collection, along with boxes from cookies, crackers, and even ice cream sandwiches, for a variety of sizes and shapes. You can cover with wrapping paper or magazine pages if you like, or use contact paper over the original packaging to infuse an Andy Warhol-inspired bit of pop art into playtime. Keep adding to the collection instead of the recycling bin.

Who Knew? Classic Tip

Make a Play-Doh substitute for your kids with an unlikely ingredient: dryer lint! First save up 3 cups of dryer lint, then stick it into a pot with 2 cups water, 1 cup flour, six to 10 drops food coloring, and ½ teaspoon vegetable or canola oil. Cook, stirring constantly, over low heat until the mixture is smooth. Then pour onto a sheet of wax paper to cool.

Play-Doh Fun Make Play-Doh play more fun with a garlic press! You may hardly ever find yourself using the designer garlic press you got for your wedding, but your kids will love it to make Play-Doh "hair." Plus, you'll finally get a chance to act out teenage fantasies of bright blue Mohawks and the like. When you're tired of playing hairdresser, use the press to revert to the usual Play-Doh noodles or worms.

Cheap Fun That Lasts for Hours If your young child likes building toys but you don't want to pay for expensive blocks, buy plastic cups in several different colors and use those instead. They're extremely cheap and just as fun to knock down!

Homemade Glitter If your kids need glitter in an emergency (and who hasn't had a glitter emergency?), you can make your own at home. Just take a cup of salt, add 10 to 15 drops of your favorite food coloring, and mix it thoroughly. Microwave on high for two to three minutes, then spread it out on a sheet of nonstick foil or wax paper to dry. If you don't use it all right away, make sure to store it in an airtight container.

Free Bath Toys If you're looking for a cheap and practical toy for kids, thoroughly wash old ketchup, salad dressing, and shampoo bottles and let the kids use them to play in the swimming pool or bathtub. They're also a good way to wash shampoo out of hair at bath time.

Flip a Flip-Flop Lost a flip-flop? Might as well put the remaining shoe to good use. Trace a fun shape in the foam flop, then cut it out with an X-Acto knife. Now your kid has a brand-new stamp great for dipping in paints and ink!

A, B, C Cards Make alphabet cards for your toddler from old catalogs and magazines. Find a picture for each letter. Using index cards, write the letter on one side with a thick marker and glue the accompanying picture on the reverse. You can go with the ubiquitous A is for apple, B is for Boat, or come up with something more inventive (A is for Android?).

Turn Markers into Watercolor Paints! If your kids are budding Picassos and Georgia O'Keeffes, you'll love this crafty tip for making your own paints on the cheap! Rather than shopping for store-bought paints, reuse old dried-up markers: Simply gather colored markers into batches by color, and tie them together with a rubber band. Pour water into small glass jars (baby food jars are perfect), and fill to just below their screw-top necks. Place the markers tip-ends down into the jars, so the inky points are soaking in the water. Leave the markers to soak overnight, and voilà—beautiful, vivid color paints!

How to Make Moon Sand If your kids like Moon Sand, that soft sand that can be molded into all kinds of shapes, here's an inexpensive version you can make yourself. Mix together 2 cups sand, 1 cup cornstarch, and ½ cup water. Kids can use their beach toys as molds, or you can provide them with cookie cutters, measuring cups, and other baking tools that they can fill to make their sand creations. (For a larger quantity, double or triple the recipe.)

Who Knew? Classic Tip

Here's a quick, homemade toy that will keep your boys busy for hours, if not days: Take a large piece of corrugated cardboard and cut it in the shape of a sword (use two pieces and tape them together, if necessary). Wrap the handle with electrical tape and the "blade" with duct tape. Your kids can practice their fencing skills against each other, and since they're playing with cardboard, you won't have to worry about them getting hurt.

Make Your Own Shrinky Dinks Who doesn't love Shrinky Dinks? For the uninitiated, they're plastic sheets of animals and other designs that kids color and decorate. The pieces are then baked in the oven until the plastic shrinks down to a tiny size. We've discovered that you can use No.

6 plastic to make your own version! Usually you'll find this kind of plastic used for take-out containers or for packaging pastries in clamshells at the supermarket. First cut the plastic into the shape that you want. Then, using sandpaper, sand down one side to make it somewhat rough. Allow your child to draw his or her desired picture or image on the rough side, and stick it in a 350° oven for about three minutes or until it shrinks down. (Keep a close eye on it. After all, watching it is the fun part!) Remove and allow to cool.

DIY Décor

Your Cup of Tea If you're into the shabby chic look, a broken teacup or mug makes a pretty container for a small plant, herb, or candle. You can use tea lights for candles or fill with melted wax topped by a cotton wick. Attach the saucer to the bottom with superglue and you have an instant conversation piece as well.

Brighten Up the Bookshelf If you're looking for an easy, inexpensive way to add a pop of color to a room, look no further than the bookshelf. You can paint the interior back "wall" of the bookshelf a color that either contrasts or coordinates with your décor. It will add a modern touch for not a lot of money!

Placemat Turned Coaster Buying new placemats doesn't mean having to get rid of the old ones. Cut them into several squares and use them as coasters! They'll protect your furniture in style, and they're easy to clean! (Just throw in the washing machine.)

Who Knew? Classic Tip

To perk up your bedroom with a splash of color, get crafty with a DIY faux-headboard. Find a colorful sheet that complements the décor of your room; any fabric will work, so consider cotton, linen, velvet, and even fur! First, consider the width of your bed; a headboard should be slightly wider than your mattress. Then decide what style of headboard you like best, and cut your fabric to the right size and shape. Either wrap your fabric around a foam base and hang it on the wall, or hang it up on its own.

A Gift for Decoration Dress up an inexpensive set of plastic drawers by covering them in wrapping paper. Choose some paper you love (you can even pick several coordinating designs), and cut the pieces to fit the size of the drawers. Then spread a crafting glue/sealer, such as Mod Podge, on the plastic and smooth the wrapping paper onto it, being careful to eliminate bubbles. Allow to dry, and apply a coat of sealant on top. Not only does the paper look beautiful, but it also hides the contents of the drawers, making everything appear neat and tidy.

Add Some Sporty Spice For the child who loves all things sports, create a unique valance he'll love using sports jerseys. Purchase several (on sale!) jerseys for whatever sport your child is into, and then hang them, one next to the other, across the length of a drapery rod. Or use old jerseys that he's grown out of!

Fun Addition to a Child's Room Here's a great decorating idea for a child's room: Make a magnetic chalkboard out of the wall! This can be easily accomplished by purchasing a can of magnetic paint and a can of chalkboard paint, both of which should be available at your local hardware store and will run you about $15 to $25 apiece. Mark off the area that you're going to paint with masking tape, and remember that it can be any shape or size. Then paint several layers of the magnetic paint, waiting for each layer to dry before adding another layer on top of it. Finally, paint on a layer of the chalkboard paint and let it

who knew? THE BIG QUESTION

Flower Arrangements

How do I make fresh flowers last longer?
—Alyssa Boyne Mills, via Facebook

What do I do if the vase I have is too big for my bouquet of flowers? **—Eli McGovern, via Twitter**

Bloom Booster Extend the life of cut flowers with a little hydrogen peroxide. Just add a capful to the vase before you put the bouquet in it. The peroxide will keep bacteria away from the flowers' stems.

Keep Away from Fruit When deciding where to place that beautiful bouquet you just brought home, steer clear of the fruit bowl. Ethylene gas given off by fruit will cause the flowers to die more quickly. Choose a spot farther away from any fruit, and your flowers will last longer.

Spud Bud A beautiful bouquet can look mediocre if the individual stems fall all around the vase. Keep them standing straight by poking holes into half a potato, sticking it in a vase, and "planting" the stems. The starch is good for the flowers too.

Berry Straight Keep flowers standing straight in a vase by slipping the stems through the holes in a berry basket. If you can't fit the entire basket in the vase, cut as much as will easily fit.

sit for two to three days. With the help of some magnets, you'll be able to hang your child's artwork on the wall, and she'll be able to doodle to her heart's delight.

Plastic Cup String Lanterns Here's a creative decorating project for kids and adults alike: You'll need string lights, plastic cups, and various art supplies. First, decorate the plastic cups with colored markers, paints, glitter, googly eyes, or any other fun embellishments you can find at a craft store. Then, poke one light bulb into the bottom of each cup, so the light illuminates the cup from the inside. You'll have a beautiful string of lanterns to hang in the playroom, a kid's bedroom, the living room, hallway, or along a staircase.

Find a Home for Buttons Buttons that have popped off and long since lost their owners make neat decorations for a plain frame. Simply use a hot-glue gun to jazz up the edges and add a personal aesthetic. (Don't forget about the extra buttons that come with fancy clothing and inevitably end up in a drawer untouched for decades.)

Delightful Decór For an easy, inexpensive decoration that looks great in any room, frame cloth napkins. Use family heirlooms, or find some beautiful designs suitable for framing at stores like World Market, Pier 1, or Target. Place them in some square frames and hang them in a row.

Family Time Big wall space to fill? Place a clock in the center of your wall, and circle it with 12 photo frames, each one placed where the hour would be. For example, you can put a wedding photo at 12:00, a picture of your child at 1:00, Grandma at 2:00, and so on. It will look great and be a fun way to display family memories.

Who Knew? Classic Tip

A fun and vintage-looking decoration for a kitchen is framed seed packets. Dig through whatever is available at your gardening store, then carefully slit the top to let the seeds loose. Center the empty pack on a matte or solid-color background, then glue with rubber cement or white glue. Frame, then hang on the wall for a perfectly themed picture.

Rev Up a Rug Give new life to a boring mudroom or entryway rug with spray paint! You'll need painter's tape, a can of primer spray paint, and your desired spray paint colors. First, spray a coat or two of primer on the rug to prep the area. Next, spray the rug your desired base color.

(You may need to apply more than one coat to cover up the rug's original color.) Once the base coat dries, use the painter's tape to create patterns, like stripes, diamonds, or chevrons, and then spray a contrasting color on top. Remove the tape, and you'll have a fun new rug.

Private Time It's great to have a bathroom with a window—it lets in lots of fresh air and light—but sometimes you want a little extra privacy. Instead of buying a frosted privacy window, pick up a bottle of a product called Gallery Glass at your local craft store. Start by cleaning the window you'd like to treat, removing any traces of dirt or residue. Then begin to squeeze the product on the inside of the window in a swirl pattern, until it's completely covered. It will look like you've covered the window in white glue, but don't worry, it will dry to a translucent finish. Allow to cure for approximately a week, then enjoy your new frosted window!

Homemade Gifts

Fancy Journals Stray beads and pieces of broken jewelry can be salvaged even if you're not into making jewelry. All you need is a hot-glue gun to add a personal touch to a plain journal. If you want to make a gift for a friend, use the beads to write the friend's name on the front of the journal. Add glitter, sequins, and anything else that will make it extra special.

Who Knew? Classic Tip

Soaps never seem to lose their appeal as gifts. They're useful and don't add clutter to people's houses (something we're always trying to avoid in ours). You can make your own by grating white, unscented soap it into a bowl with warm water. For color, add a few drops of food coloring appropriate for the holiday. Next, add a drop or two of an essential oil (lavender or rose are lovely) then knead like pizza dough and make into little balls. As an alternative, use candy molds for fun shapes. Leave them to dry on wax paper for a day or so.

Christmas Gift Go-to Are there any soda lovers on your gift list? How about beer drinkers? This clever holiday gift is perfect for any of them! Buy a six-pack of soda, root beer, or real beer in pretty glass bottles—we love the fancy vintage-looking soda bottles. Then turn each bottle into an adorable reindeer: You'll need pipe cleaners for antlers, googly eyes, red pom-poms for the nose, colored ribbon, and a hot-glue gun. Bend the pipe cleaners into antler shapes and attach them to the back of the reindeer's "head" (i.e., the neck of the bottle). Glue on the eyes and nose, then tie a ribbon around the front of the bottle just under the nose—a simple knot here will resemble a reindeer mouth. Rudolph never looked so delicious!

Holiday Gift Idea Looking for an easy, heartfelt (but inexpensive) holiday gift? How about a personalized calendar of your children's artwork? Pick up free calendars distributed by local companies, then paste drawings or paintings from the past year on top of each month's image. Your kids will feel proud of their work, and their grandparent, uncle, or godparent will love their new calendar.

Turn Buttons into Hair Accessories Here's a little project we like to call "Buttonovation." If you have spare fabric buttons lying around (or if you have an old buttoned blazer that's no longer wearable save for the cute buttons), you can recycle them as stylish accessories! Transform a button into a hair tie by looping an elastic hair band through the notch on the back; knot it around the notch, and voila! Or make a hairpin by sliding a bobby pin through that same back notch.

Gift for a Bride-to-Be Here's a wonderful, one-of-a-kind gift for a bridal shower: Buy a blank hardcover book, add dividers, and create a family cookbook. Just ask the bride and groom's families to provide their favorite treasured recipes.

Gift Basket Baskets that strawberries and other berries come in are perfect for presents. Thread ribbon through a berry basket, line it with wrapping paper, and use it as a gift basket for your little one to bring a few muffins to a new neighbor or friend.

Who Knew? Classic Tip

Turn your gift packaging into part of the gift itself. For a bridal shower, wrap your gift with a pretty bath, kitchen, or tea towel. Write a recipe onto the gift tag, or use a recipe card *for* the tag, and tie a bow with a beautiful ribbon and a kitchen utensil, such as salad tongs, inserted inside.

Perfect Box for Baked Goods If you like to bake goodies as gifts, consider reusing empty aluminum foil and plastic wrap boxes as gift boxes. Cover the box in festive gift wrap, line the inside with tissue paper, and stick your treats inside. They're the perfect size for some cupcakes or muffins!

Make Your Own Cards Show your friends you care and save money by making your own cards to send for birthdays or other occasions. Look through old magazines for funny photos (or shots of your friend's celebrity crush) to use for the front. Or for something more complicated, visit Card-Making-World.com for ideas and free backgrounds and embellishments to download.

Special Delivery Mailing a card and want to do something creative for that extra-special touch? Visit your local coin and stamp dealer to find unique, vintage postage sold at face value or less. Many dealers sell old yet valid stamps that aren't worth much to collectors, so you're likely to find a bargain on cool, old-fashioned postage.

Dollar Bill Designs Instead of doling out cash for fancy bows to decorate gifts, use your actual dollars to make the bows. Fold a dollar bill (or more, if you're a high roller) accordion-style and affix with a ribbon over a wrapped gift. Kids will love it!

See Also . . . For DIY cosmetics like face masks and toners, check out the Better Beauty Ideas chapter!

chapter 11

Better Beauty Ideas

Luxurious Skin Treatments

Milk and Cookies Bath This soothing and exfoliating oatmeal bath smells like warm cookies—without the extra calories! In a food processor, pulse together ½ cup oats with 3 tablespoons powdered milk, 3 tablespoons baking soda, and ¼ teaspoon ground cinnamon. Pour the powder into running bath water, and enjoy.

Buttermilk for Beauty If you're like us, you never seem to use up an entire carton of buttermilk after buying it for a recipe. Luckily, there's a second use for it: Keep your skin looking young by dabbing it on brown spots or other discolorations. A study recently found that people saw big improvements in their skin after dabbing it on spots each night for three months. Leave on for 10 minutes before rinsing.

She's Got Legs Did you know that the time of day that you shave your legs matters? For the smoothest legs, shave in the morning. By evening, legs tend to be more swollen, making it harder for your razor to get as close to the skin.

Help for Varicose Veins Varicose veins are one of the most annoying signs of aging. To temporarily reduce their appearance, soak some paper towels in witch hazel, a powerful astringent, and wrap the towels around your legs. Remove after five minutes. This tip works best after showering when the pores are open.

Who Knew? Classic Tip

Here's an easy way to have a relaxing soak in a bath without having to buy bath salts. Just place one or two green tea bags under the faucet as you fill up your bath. The antioxidants in the tea will leave your skin feeling fresh.

Erase Age Spots If you're looking to eliminate unsightly age spots, sometimes you have to get serious! That means whipping up this stinky solution that works better than anything else we've ever tried. Grate a medium onion onto a cheesecloth or sturdy paper towel, then squeeze the onion juice into a bowl. Mix in 1 tablespoon each of white vinegar and hydrogen peroxide. Dab the mixture on the age spots, twice a day (keeping away from your eyes), and keep it in the fridge when you're not using it. You should see results in a week or two!

Tender Loving Care, Everywhere You may be overlooking the number one spot on your body that needs regular exfoliation! Make sure to spend a minute or two every week to exfoliate your underarms, which can be prone to ingrown hairs and residues caused from antiperspirants and deodorants. Use your favorite facial exfoliant, or use a mixture of brown sugar and olive oil. Massage into armpits and wash away to make your skin even and healthy.

Banish B.O. with Baking Soda Sure, you've used baking soda to eliminate odors in your refrigerator, but have you ever used it to freshen up, well, you? Let's be honest: When hot weather arrives, we can all feel a little not-so-fresh. Try adding a half cup or so of baking soda to your bath water a few times a week whenever you've been sweating a lot. It helps eliminate the bacteria that cause odor all over your body, not just under your arms.

Manicures, Pedicures and Other Tips for Hands and Feet

Easy French Manicures at Home If you've ever wanted to do an at-home French manicure, but had no clue how to get those perfect crescent shapes at the top of your nails, we've got an incredible tip for you! All you need is a plastic bandage wide enough to cover your nail. Stick the end of the bandage on your nail, exposing just the amount you want to paint. Then apply the polish, and move the bandage on to the next nail. Now the only thing left to do is wait for your nails to dry—and show them off!

Who Knew? Classic Tip

You have just enough time to touch up your nails before you leave but not long enough to dry them. Make your nail polish dry more quickly by spraying your final coat with cooking spray. The oil will help them dry faster, and it will moisturize your cuticles too!

Nail Polish Protection Painting your nails at home? For a salon-fresh look, first apply petroleum jelly to your cuticles and to the skin around your nails. When the polish is dry, wipe away the jelly along with any stray polish on your skin.

Spit Shine You just got a perfect pedicure at the salon, and suddenly you bump your toe against the leg of a chair, smudging the polish. Before you get too upset, quickly lick one of your fingers and run it over the smudged nail, applying a bit of pressure if needed. Surprisingly, there's a chemical in saliva that reacts with nail polish and can smooth over these little mishaps.

Gone Dotty Spice up your manicure with some polka dots! Make them perfect with this fun trick: Unbend a bobby pin, dip one tip into the nail polish, and then dot it on your nails. It's so easy you'll want dotted nails all the time!

Who Knew? Classic Tip

Try this homemade cuticle cream and you'll give up the store-bought variety forever: Mix 2 tablespoons each of olive oil and petroleum jelly along with the zest of half an orange. Store in the refrigerator, and apply at bedtime for soft, lovely-smelling nails.

A Fungus Among Us If you have an unsightly nail fungus that makes you want to hide your hands or feet from view, you'll love this tip. Soak your nails in a mixture of 1 cup vinegar and 2 cups warm water every day for 15 minutes. The acid in the vinegar will attack the fungus, leaving you with lovelier nails. You can also try this tip for athlete's foot.

Nail Fungus Fighter To help get rid of unsightly nail fungus, try this home remedy: Rub a mentholated vapor rub, like Vicks, on the nail twice a day. If used consistently, it should eliminate the fungus.

Brighten Your Nails If dark nail polish has stained your fingernails, here's a quick fix: Plop a denture-cleaning tablet into a glass of water and soak your nails for a couple of minutes. The stain will come right off.

Try a Little Tenderness The next time you buy a pineapple at the supermarket, don't just toss the peel. Use it on your feet! Pineapple contains bromelain, a natural meat tenderizer, which is also great at exfoliating rough spots on your skin like your heels and elbows. Rub the fleshy side of the pineapple peel against your skin for several minutes, then rinse.

Strawberry Scrub Try this fresh strawberry scrub to exfoliate and remove dry skin, particularly on trouble spots like the feet, hands, and elbows. Mash 1 cup strawberries with 1 tablespoon olive oil and 1 tablespoon salt. Massage onto skin, leave for a few minutes, then rinse. The strawberries and salt will slough the dry skin away, and the oil will provide lasting moisture.

Callus Buster When spring comes around, it's time to start paying attention to those feet you've neglected all winter. To soften calluses and get your feet ready for sandal season, use an old-fashioned standby: castor oil. Before turning in for the night, rub castor oil into the problem spots on your feet, then cover with socks. Repeat nightly for a week to reveal soft, smooth skin.

Who Knew? Classic Tip

Banish corns with an onion compress. Soak a slice of onion in apple cider vinegar for a few hours. Remove it and place the onion over the corn, covering with a bandage. Put on cotton socks to protect the area and leave overnight.

Can the Corns Painful corns can put a cramp in your style, especially in the summer. Flatten them with this easy tip. All you need are bandages, petroleum jelly, and an emery board. Every night before you go to sleep rub a little petroleum jelly on the corns and cover with a bandage. Then, in the morning, file the corns gently with the emery board. Repeat the process every night until they're gone, usually in about 10 to 14 days, and make sure not to use the emery board for any other purpose, like filing your nails.

Beat Sweaty Feet Like most people, our feet get really stinky in the summer months. Lucky for us (and the people around us), we've discovered a simple trick to prevent and fight foot odor and the sweat that causes it: cornstarch! Just sprinkle some in your socks before you put them on. Cornstarch is a great way to prevent blisters too!

Make Your Face Fabulous

Rice Face Wash Everyone knows that rice is a nutrient-rich and delicious food, but did you know that it's also an excellent addition to your skin-care regimen? Loaded with vitamins B and E, the grain will smooth and soften skin when used as a daily face wash. All you'll need is uncooked white rice and water: Boil ½ cup rice in 2 cups water. Take out the rice and let the water cool down. Use a cloth to massage the rice water onto your skin, and rinse.

Steam Clean This super-effective pore cleanser couldn't be simpler. Place three bags of chamomile tea in a medium-size bowl, and cover with several cups boiling water. Cover the bowl with a towel, and allow the tea to steep for 10 minutes. Then remove the towel, place it over your head, and hold your face over the bowl for about five minutes.

The steam will open your pores, and the chamomile will help unclog them.

Kiwifruit Facial Scrub Who knew you could make a revitalizing facial scrub with a kiwifruit? Peel and mash the kiwi (or puree it in the food processor) with 3 tablespoons cornmeal, then scrub it on clean skin. The vitamin C from the kiwi will help brighten skin, and the little seeds and cornmeal will remove dead skin cells.

Champagne Scrub Have a teeny bit of champagne or white wine left after a party? Make a face scrub with it! Wine contains tartaric acid, a terrific exfoliant. Mix a few teaspoons sugar with enough wine to make a paste, then massage into clean skin.

Nourish with Nutmeg This nutmeg-milk scrub provides a double whammy of skin nourishment: Nutmeg works as an astringent, exfoliant, and anti-inflammatory (good-bye blackheads and acne), while the milk's lactic acid works as a peel to eliminate dead skin cells. To make the scrub, combine nutmeg and milk until the mixture resembles a paste. After washing your face with a cleanser, massage the nutmeg scrub onto your skin in gentle circular strokes. Exfoliate for five to 10 minutes, then rinse.

Thyme for Toner It's long been known that fennel seeds can reduce puffiness and skin irritation, and that thyme has antiseptic and astringent properties. Here's how to use both to make a gentle facial toner. You'll need 2 sprigs fresh thyme (or 1½ teaspoons dried), 2 teaspoons fennel seeds, ½ cup boiling water, and 1 tablespoon freshly squeezed lemon juice. First, strip the leaves from the sprigs of fresh thyme, and crush the fennel seeds in a mortar and pestle. Place both herbs in a bowl with the boiling water and lemon juice. Cover, and allow the mixture to steep for 20 minutes. Strain the toner into a jar, and store in the refrigerator for up to two weeks. Apply the cool mixture with cotton balls to clean skin to soothe redness and tighten pores. You won't believe how great your skin feels!

Green Tea Facial Spray Freshen up your face with an easy green tea mist! Place two green tea bags in a spray bottle filled with water and allow to steep for several hours. Store the bottle in the refrigerator, and mist on your face whenever you need a little refreshment. Not only will the mist feel great, but the green tea will also nourish the skin with essential antioxidants.

For Sumptuous Skin Turmeric and besan (also called chickpea flour or gram flour) are centuries-old magic ingredients in the Indian woman's skin-care regimen. They

who knew? THE BIG QUESTION

Getting Rid of Blackheads

What are some natural remedies for getting rid of blackheads? **—Jessica Davila, via Facebook**

Blackhead Chaser Getting rid of blackheads can be frustrating, but lime juice can help. Mix together 2 tablespoons salt and 2 tablespoons lime juice. Spread the paste onto clean skin and allow to dry, then rinse off with warm water. This wonderful smelling toner will not only get rid of blackheads, it will tighten your pores!

Egg on Your Face For eliminating blackheads, egg whites are egg-cellent (sorry, we couldn't resist). Whisk an egg white, and apply it directly to the face. Cover the area with toilet paper, and allow it to dry until the paper becomes stiff. Then peel it away, and rinse with warm water.

Gelatin Pore Strips Pore strips like Bioré work great for blackheads, but they're expensive. Here's an affordable alternative to commercial pore strips: Mix together 1 to 2 tablespoons unflavored gelatin with equal parts milk, and heat until warm. Spread this mixture on your skin, and allow to dry completely. You will be able to peel it off in strips, removing blackheads in the process!

brighten skin tone, clear up acne and redness, and help reduce signs of aging. They're also easily found in Indian grocery stores. To make this scrumptious mask, combine 1 tablespoon chickpea flour, 1 tablespoon milk, and 1/8 teaspoon turmeric. You can also add a bit of sandalwood powder for fragrance. Apply the mixture to your face. Leave it on for 15 minutes, then rinse. Do this once or twice a week and you won't believe how wonderful your face feels!

Pretty as a Peach For an easy, beautifying facial mask, puree the flesh of one peach with a splash of brandy. Spread the mixture onto clean skin, and wait 20 minutes before rinsing with warm water. It will make your skin feel great, and smell good while doing it!

Luxe Firming Copper Mask Copper, a popular ingredient in expensive anti-aging skin products, helps to firm and smooth skin, as recent research shows. Fortunately, one of the most copper-rich foods just happens to be chocolate! Here's a great facial mask that takes advantage of the antioxidant and anti-aging qualities of chocolate and copper. Plus, it smells divine! Combine 2 tablespoons unsweetened cocoa powder with enough milk or heavy cream to make a paste. Apply to the skin, and leave for 15 minutes, then rinse with warm water.

Cool as a Cucumber Here's a unique twist on the traditional cucumber-slices-on-eyes trick. Peel and chop half a cucumber and puree it in a blender with ½ cup cold water. Strain the mixture into a spray bottle. Spritz it onto round cosmetic pads to saturate, and place the pads on your eyes for 10 minutes. Do this anytime you have some extra redness or puffiness around the eyes for immediate relief!

Minty-Fresh Eye Treatment If you're like us, you're no stranger to long busy days and late busy nights. And, also like us, you might have that wear and tear written right on your face—in those dark, saggy rings under your eyes. To fight these, we've found that a sprig of fresh mint leaves can do the trick: Chop up and crush the mint, then pat it onto the dark skin beneath your eyes. Let it sit for about 20 minutes, and rinse.

See Also . . . For facial treatments that are especially for the treatment of acne, see the Natural Remedies and First Aid chapter.

Keep Your Brows in Line If you can't convince your husband to trim his giant eyebrows, you at least might have some luck getting him to keep unruly hairs in line! Just use an old toothbrush, but make it extra effective by spraying it with hair spray first. Then comb over brows to tame any wild hairs and rinse the brush after using.

Pucker Up For lips that need a little extra TLC, especially in the winter, try this effective scrub. Mix together 2 teaspoons baking soda with enough lemon juice to make a paste. Gently scrub the mixture over your lips with a dry toothbrush for a minute or two, then rinse, and apply some petroleum jelly or your favorite lip balm.

Who Knew? Classic Tip

To whiten your teeth naturally (and cheaply), mash four to five strawberries with ½ teaspoon baking soda. Brush onto your teeth with a toothbrush and let sit for 10 to 15 minutes. Then rinse out and brush your teeth as usual, making sure no strawberry seeds got caught between your teeth. Repeat this process every night and you'll start to see results in three to four weeks.

Lip-Smacking Scrub Eliminate unsightly rough spots and help lipstick adhere more evenly by applying an exfoliating lip scrub. This homemade version is easy, and so tasty you may just want to eat it! Mash together a strawberry or two with a drizzle of honey. Rub the mixture on your lips in a circular motion, and wait five minutes before rinsing (or licking!) off.

Use the Whole Tube of Toothpaste To get every bit of toothpaste out of the tube, soak the nearly empty tube in a cup of hot water for several minutes. It will loosen the remaining toothpaste from the sides of the tube, and you'll be able to brush a few more times before having to buy more. Every penny counts!

Healthy Hair and Scalp

Coconut-Citrus Scalp Rub To soothe a dry, itchy scalp, try this terrific-smelling treatment. Mix together ¼ cup coconut oil with 3 tablespoons lemon or lime juice. Massage the mixture into your scalp, and leave on for 15 to 20 minutes. Rinse, and follow with your regular shampoo and conditioner. You'll love the way your scalp feels, and how your hair smells!

Eggs for Hair Your hair's unexpected best friend? Eggs. Just beat two or three eggs together in a bowl and apply to damp hair, making sure to massage into your scalp. Let sit for 20 minutes, then rinse with cool water and your hair will never feel more conditioned. If you suffer from oily scalp, use egg whites only, and if you have dry or brittle hair, use only egg yolks.

Seal Your Split Ends Your hairstylist just called to reschedule your appointment, but you've just had it with your split ends! This simple moisturizing hair mask will rescue your locks and buy you a few days until you can get yourself into the salon chair. Whisk together an egg yolk with 1 tablespoon grapeseed or olive oil and 1 tablespoon honey. Massage the mixture through damp hair, paying special attention to the ends. Then cover hair with a towel or plastic wrap, and wait 30 minutes. Rinse with warm water.

Sweeten Up Your Hair Dye If at-home hair dyes irritate your scalp, try adding a little Sweet 'N Low to the mixture before applying it. The artificial sweetener helps neutralize any ammonia-based formula. It will be easier on your scalp while still being just as effective.

Banish Buildup with Beer The next time you have some flat beer around the house, use it in your hair! Beer acts as a clarifying agent to remove product buildup that's left behind by conditioners, gels, mousses, and other styling products. Mix together ¼ cup beer with 1 cup warm water, pour over your hair in the shower, and rub in well, then rinse. Just don't forget to shampoo and condition afterward to make sure you don't leave the house smelling like a frat party!

Skip the Scalp Save money and add volume to your hair by using conditioner only on the ends of your hair. When you apply conditioner to the roots, it can unnecessarily weigh down your locks and make hair appear greasy. Plus, the hair closest to the scalp is newer and healthier, and less in need of extra moisture.

Who Knew? Classic Tip

Suffering from dry hair? Here's a surefire way to make it moist again. Mash a banana and mix with a teaspoon of almond or olive oil. Rub the mixture into your hair and scalp, and let sit for 20 minutes. Rinse off and shampoo and condition as usual. You'll be surprised at the results!

A Saline Solution Even if you don't have time to properly wash, dry, and style your hair, you can still get rid of oiliness in just a few minutes. Here's how: Take a handful of kosher salt and rub it into the roots and scalp. (You may want to do this in the tub or over a sink to avoid making

who knew? THE BIG QUESTION

Dandruff Remedies

How do I get rid of dandruff?

—Aaron Feeley, via email

Make Dandruff Disappear You don't have to buy expensive shampoos to get rid of dandruff. Instead, use something that's already in your medicine cabinet—mouthwash. After shampooing your hair, pour a solution of half mouthwash, half water over it. Work into your scalp and let sit for five minutes, then rinse out and condition as usual. Repeat once or twice a week until dandruff is gone.

Keep Dandruff Away with Aspirin Aspirin may help reduce dandruff if you crush a couple of tablets and add them to your normal shampoo. Just make sure to let the shampoo sit on your hair for one to two minutes before washing it out.

Natural Dandruff Remedy You can also use apple cider vinegar to regulate the acid level on your scalp and clear out the flakes. Maximize the benefits by adding fresh mint! Heat ¼ cup apple cider vinegar with ½ cup water and a few leaves of fresh mint in the microwave or over low heat on the stove. Let cool, then chill in the fridge overnight. Tomorrow use it to cover your scalp—massaging the mixture into your hair—and wait a half hour before you shampoo it out.

a mess.) Wait five minutes so that the salt can absorb the oil, then shake it out. The effect is similar to—but much cheaper than—those dry shampoos on the market.

Who Knew? Classic Tip

To get soft, shiny hair, use olive oil. Rub into dry hair, starting at the ends and working at least halfway up. Then blow-dry on the hottest setting and let sit for at least 30 minutes. Wash and condition as usual, but get ready for some super-sleek locks!

Shampoo Less Often Here's a great trick for those of us with oily hair who want to extend the time between shampoos. Spray freshly shampooed hair with a mixture of equal parts apple cider vinegar and water. Comb it through the hair, and wait a few minutes before rinsing it out and styling as usual. The acid in the vinegar helps keep oily hair cleaner longer!

Pump Up the Volume Here's an amazing hair treatment to add volume to flat hair—you won't believe it till you try it! All you need is your usual conditioner and some Epsom salts, which are available at most drugstores. Squirt some of the conditioner into a microwave-safe bowl, then add an equal amount of Epsom salts. Mix together, then heat in the microwave on high for 30 seconds, stirring halfway through. Continue microwaving in 15-second increments until it's warm, which will help your hair absorb the treatment. Shampoo and rinse your hair as usual, then add the Epsom salts–conditioner mixture to your hair and let sit for 15 minutes before rinsing. You'll love how bouncy and beautiful your hair is when it dries!

Who Knew? Classic Tip

If you have dark hair, you can conceal grays without having to pay for hair dye. Just rinse your hair with strong coffee (let it cool first!). Let the coffee sit in your hair for three minutes, then rinse out. Repeat one or two times as necessary. The coffee will not only provide a subtle tint, it will also get rid of any product buildup on your locks!

Shine On For shiny locks, it's baking soda to the rescue! Add a tablespoon of baking soda to your normal amount of shampoo in the shower, and your hair will be smooth and lustrous.

For Beachy, Wavy Hair For that just-off-the-beach look, try this simple DIY salt spray that will cost you virtually nothing. In a spray bottle, combine a teaspoon or so of salt with warm water, and shake until fully dissolved. Then spray all over damp hair and style as usual. The salt acts as a natural volumizer, resulting in perfectly tousled waves, without a trip to the ocean—or an expensive styling product.

Clean Your Hair Clips Hair accessories can accumulate dirt and oils left by sprays, gels, and other products as well as your natural oils and sweat. To keep clips, combs, bobby pins, barrettes, and ties in tip-top shape, wash them regularly in the dishwasher! We usually just throw ours in with the silverware.

Keep Bobby Pins in Place To keep your bobby pins in place all day, spray them with a little hair spray before using. The stickiness will stop them from falling out of your hair.

Makeup Matters

Lighten the Load If you're preparing for a special evening out and will only be carrying a small clutch, you probably won't have much room to bring makeup. Instead, grab a few Ziploc bags—the small snack size is ideal here—and some cotton swabs. Dip each swab into the make-up you'll be wearing that night, whether it's lipstick, eye shadow, or blush, and put each swab into its own bag. You'll be able to freshen up, and still have room in your clutch for your keys and driver's license!

Who Knew? Classic Tip

To avoid getting lipstick on your teeth, after you apply, close your mouth over your finger and slowly pull it out. This will save you time and time again!

From Loss to Gloss Save a too-dark lipstick from a lifetime in the back of the makeup drawer by turning it into a lighter lip gloss. In a small bowl, heat a little petroleum jelly in the microwave until it is warm. (Try five to 10 seconds to start.) Then stir in a piece of your lipstick, and combine until well-blended. If it's still too dark, add a little more petroleum jelly. Once you're satisfied with the shade, transfer it to a small container or tin for storage.

Looking for Lipstick? To find your ideal lip color, purse your lips together tightly for 30 seconds, then release and take a look in the mirror. Look for a color that matches that slightly deepened shade. Like your lips, only better!

Ditch a Double Chin If a double chin is driving you nuts, use a little makeup to hide it. When applying powder or foundation to your face, use a slightly darker shade under your chin, which will make it appear to recede. Blend toward the back of the jawline to add definition.

Who Knew? Classic Tip

Applying the finishing touches to your makeup and realize you're out of mascara? Here's a great tip to get that last bit out of the tube. Simply roll the tube quickly between your hands for 30 seconds. The heat generated by the friction is enough to soften the mascara stuck to the sides of the tube, so you'll have just enough to apply to your lashes before you run out the door.

Magic Eyelash Wand When you toss an old tube of mascara, don't throw away the wand! It can become a valuable tool in your makeup arsenal. Clean it with warm soapy water, then use it to separate lashes stuck together with mascara. Or, add a bit of petroleum jelly to the wand, as apply as you would mascara to moisturize dry lashes.

No More Mascara Mess Tired of getting mascara on your skin when you apply it to your lower lashes? Next time, grab a plastic spoon and gently place it under the lower lashes, with the curved side facing out. When you apply the mascara, the excess will stick to the spoon, not your face.

Mascara Miracle Mascara starting to dry out? Just add several drops of saline eyedrops and shake. The eyedrops will keep the mascara lasting much longer than you ever thought possible!

Mascara Problem, Solved If you've ever blinked while applying mascara and gotten tiny black dots under your eyes, you'll love this tip. Before you get out the mascara, place a small Post-it Note under each eye. If you blink, the mascara will get on the notes rather than your skin, and then you can pull them off and get on with your beauty regimen.

Curly Lashes to the Max Super-power your eyelash curler by running a blow dryer on high over it for 5–7 seconds before curling your lashes. The heat will help give you extra curl that will last all day!

chapter 12

Natural Remedies and First Aid

Mouth Matters

Ease Digestive Issues

Weight-Loss Wonders

Arthritis and Other
Aches and Pains

First Aid Fixes

Fighting Colds, Flus, and Sinus Problems

Sore Throat? Aspirin does more than just relieve headaches! If you have a sore throat, dissolve two noncoated tablets in a glass of water and gargle. Just be sure to note that this only works with aspirin—don't try it with other pain relievers like ibuprofen.

Do Some Jell-O Shots! Sore throat slowing you down? Here's a tasty way to soothe it that you and the kids will love! Prepare Jell-O according to the directions, but instead of sticking it in the refrigerator to set, put some in a mug, and heat it in the microwave with a squirt of honey. When you drink the warm mixture, the gelatin will coat and soothe your throat, and the honey will help kill germs. Watch out with this one though, or the kids will start playing sick just to get some liquid Jell-O!

Sore Throat Soother If you're looking for a miracle cure for a sore throat, it's oil of oregano, which you can add to water and gargle. This amazing oil (from a different oregano plant that produces the common spice) is great for any respiratory problem and can also be applied topically to athlete's foot or other fungal infections. It's also been known to help teething babies when a drop is applied to their gums!

Who Knew? Classic Tip

Sore throat? Here's a great lemon remedy: Gargle with one part lemon juice and one part warm water. Lemon helps fight bacteria and soothes your throat.

Stuffy Nose Solution Got the sniffles? You can clear up a stuffy nose without making a trip to the medicine aisle. Just pop a couple strong mints (like Altoids) in your mouth instead—the potent peppermint will help clear your sinuses and also soothe any irritation in your throat.

Warming Socks If you have a cold that's been hanging around forever, try this remedy to rid yourself of congestion once and for all—while you sleep! Get a pair of cotton socks damp, but not dripping, with cold water. You can even put them in the freezer for a couple minutes to make them extra cold. Put them on, and then put a pair of dry wool socks on over them. Go to bed immediately. As you sleep, the heat from your upper body will be drawn down to your feet, allowing the congestion in your head

who knew? THE BIG QUESTION

Getting Rid of Allergens

My allergies are driving me crazy this year! Are there any easy ways to decrease the amount of allergens that get into my house?

—Kevin Li, via Facebook

Mind the Mold Spores If you're prone to nasal allergies, be sure your houseplants aren't contributing to the problem. Many potted plants give off mold spores, thanks to damp soil, but you can reduce this risk by choosing varieties that don't need a lot of water like cacti, jade plants, and dragon tree.

Keep Spores Out If you're allergic to mold, your allergies could be triggered by spores that float in through your windows and get stuck on windowsills, creating even more mold spores. Keep them away with the help of a candle. Just rub a white candle on your windowsill to create a transparent barrier that will keep mold and mildew from taking root.

Pummel Pollen If you have a pollen allergy, try to keep sneeze-inducing allergens out of your home. Take a shower immediately after doing any yard work to get rid of pollens you may have carried in on your hair and skin, and throw your clothes in the laundry basket. Animals can carry in pollen too. Before letting your pet inside, wipe him or her down with a wet rag or baby wipe. Showering at night can also reduce pollen on your hair and skin and help you sleep better.

to reduce. You'll also be stunned to find that your feet are warm and dry by morning.

Ease the Aches of the Flu If the flu's got you feeling sore and achy in your muscles, try using this concoction on your sore spots: Combine 1 cup olive oil with 1 tablespoon horseradish, and let sit for a half hour. Gently rub the oil mixture on your achy muscles, and you'll feel better in no time.

Who Knew? Classic Tip

If your eyes are itchy, try this quick fix to cut down on your misery: Rub a small amount of baby shampoo on your eyelids. It should reduce your symptoms dramatically.

Make it Yourself Vick's Vaporub can be a lifesaver for late-night congestion. Here's a do-it-yourself version that has all of the benefits without any of the chemicals: Mix ¼ cup melted beeswax (available online, in health stores, or from honey purveyors) with 1 cup olive oil, 15 drops eucalyptus essential oil, and 10 drops peppermint essential oil. Pour into a small container to cool. (You may need to reheat when reusing.)

The Balloon Trick If you've ever experienced pressure in your ears during a flight, you may have chewed gum to relieve the pressure. If you have a cold or sinus pressure, this trick will help your ears in a similar way, and is especially great for kids. Just blow up a few balloons, which will increase the pressure in your sinuses and help unblock your ears.

Who Knew? Classic Tip

Oil found in raw onion is antimicrobial, which makes onions great cures for upper respiratory ailments. If you have a minor earache, onion may help. Slice a fresh onion and heat it in the microwave on high for one minute. Wrap it in cheesecloth or another thin cloth so that it doesn't burn your skin, and then hold it against the ailing ear for 20 to 30 minutes. See a doctor if the pain gets worse or continues for longer than 24 hours.

Eliminate Excess Earwax Although earwax is intended to protect your super-sensitive outer ear, too much wax can inhibit hearing, foster infection, and simply be uncomfortable. If you or your family members are prone to lots of earwax, try this easy cleaning solution. You'll need a medicine dropper or cotton balls, olive or almond oil, and hydrogen peroxide. With head tilted so the ear faces upward, place two drops of oil into the ear canal and let sit for a minute or two. Repeat with a few drops of hydrogen peroxide, and leave for about 10 minutes. When time's up and the peroxide is no longer bubbling, tip the head to the reverse side so the solution can drip out. Wipe away any drips or excess solution with cotton balls or a towel.

Putting an End to Insomnia and Fatigue

Nuts for Sleep If you have a hard time winding down at the end of the day, try eating some almonds! Rich in sleep-promoting chemicals such as tryptophan (yes, just like the Thanksgiving turkey) and magnesium, almonds are a healthy, drug-free way to help you get that much-needed shut-eye.

Always Exhausted? If you're feeling fatigued all of the time, it might not be because of lack of sleep—it could be because of the food you're eating. Food has a direct effect on your blood sugar levels, which in turn affect your body's insulin production. Short-term spikes in blood sugar can contribute to a feeling of exhaustion, and consistent blood sugar spikes over a period of several years can even contribute to diabetes and obesity. Aim to eat 90 to 120 grams of protein per day, spread evenly among meals and small snacks. Getting 30 grams of protein with breakfast, such as in a protein shake, egg white omelet, or turkey sausage is a great start to your day. Then make sure you're eating protein at lunch and dinner (a chicken breast or hamburger patty are each about 30 grams of protein). Consistent protein intake will also help stave off sugar cravings! If you feel tired in the middle of the day, sugar is actually one of the worst things you can eat. It messes with your blood sugar levels and gives you a sense of "false energy" that will only cause you to crash and burn.

Who Knew? Classic Tip

If you're having trouble sleeping, try this salty tip: At bedtime, drink a glass of water, then let a pinch of salt dissolve on your tongue, making sure it doesn't touch the roof of your mouth. Studies have shown that the combination of salt and water can induce a deep sleep.

Stop Insomnia—and Your TV Recent research has shown that staring at a backlit screen (such as a TV, computer, or smartphone) will decrease the amount of melatonin your body is producing. Since melatonin is a hormone the body produces to help you sleep, you do not want to decrease melatonin as your bedtime approaches. Set aside the TV, laptop, or video game after dinnertime. Similarly, skin exposure to light can decrease melatonin as well, which is why it's important to sleep in a completely dark room.

Help for Headaches

Stop Headaches with a Simple Change Does reading text on your computer sometimes give you a headache? Your font may be to blame. Fonts that are sans serif—meaning they don't have those final strokes at the end of each letter—are easier to read then those that aren't. Some sans serif fonts include Arial, Verdana, and Helvetica. Fonts that have serifs and should be avoided include Times New Roman, Century Gothic, and Courier.

Medicine-Free Headache Relief Next time you or your family members have a headache, pour a couple glasses of Gatorade rather than reaching for the painkillers. Gatorade replenishes the body with liquids and electrolytes, and since headaches are often caused by dehydration, the energy drink can fix the problem without the need for medicine.

Salad Days Are Here Again As soon as you feel a headache coming on, don't head for the medicine cabinet; instead try olive oil. Scientific studies have shown that just a few teaspoons of olive oil eaten at the onset of a headache can have an anti-inflammatory effect, reducing pain as well as ibuprofen does.

Who Knew? Classic Tip

An old-fashioned and effective way to treat headaches is to cut a lime in half and rub it on your forehead. In a few minutes, the throbbing should subside.

Tension Tamer If you're prone to tension headaches, you may be unconsciously clenching your jaw when you're stressed. Try paying closer attention to your body, and the next time you notice yourself clenching, gently place a pencil between your teeth and hold it. It will serve as a reminder not to bite down hard. With time, you may be able to train your jaw not to clench, thus avoiding those painful headaches. Try placing colorful notes or stickers around your desk, work area, or home to mentally remind yourself to check and see if you're stress-clenching. (Then stop!)

Solutions to Skin Problems

Ease Bruises with a Banana Bananas to the rescue! A simple way to help bruises fade fast is with a banana peel. Just apply a piece of banana peel, flesh side down, to the bruise, cover with a bandage, and leave on overnight. By the morning, the bruise will have faded.

Who Knew? Classic Tip

You had a great day on the beach, but now your back is burned to a crisp. To help ease the pain of a sunburn, rub vinegar on the affected area with a cotton ball or soft cloth. You may smell a bit like salad dressing, but your skin will immediately feel cooler.

Soothe Sunburned Skin with Papaya To gently remove dead skin cells from a peeling sunburn, apply some mashed papaya to the skin. Papaya contains papain, a natural exfoliator and anti-inflammatory agent, so it will soothe your pain and eliminate the dead skin cells. Keep the papaya on the skin for five minutes, then rinse.

who knew? THE BIG QUESTION

Acne Answers

What are some natural ways to get rid of pimples? **—Kelly DiRussa, via Facebook**

Peroxide for Pimples! Over-the-counter acne creams are effective, but there's a product in your medicine cabinet that works just as well and is much less expensive: hydrogen peroxide. Just dab a little on the blemish twice a day.

Easy Pimple Prevention If you feel a pimple sprouting up, fix it fast! Add a few drops of water to a spoonful of sugar until it makes a paste, then apply it to your pimple before you go to sleep. The sucrose in the sugar will help inhibit the growth of the pimple while reducing swelling.

Banana Peel Prescription Want to get rid of acne? Try using a banana peel! Simply rub the pulpy side of the peel onto clean skin like its lotion. It has both anti-inflammatory and anti-microbial properties.

A Vision in Visine Who knew you could use eyedrops to get rid of pimples? Put a few drops on the back of a metal spoon and place in freezer. A minute or so later, it should be ready to apply to the blemish. The eye drops takes away redness while the cold goes to work to minimize swelling.

Ginger for Burns If you sustain a minor burn in the kitchen, reach for some ginger. Cut off the end and press the exposed area against your burn. Many say ginger works even better than a piece of aloe plant at soothing burns.

Who Knew? Classic Tip

It's long been stated as fact—then disputed—that duct tape can help cure warts. It may seem strange, but medical studies have concluded that when patients cover their warts with duct tape every day for a month, 85 percent of them will see a reduction in the wart. That's compared to only a 60 percent reduction in patients who used cryotherapy (having the wart frozen off by a dermatologist). It's hard to believe, but many people swear by the treatment! Our opinion? It's worth a shot, especially if you don't have health insurance.

Warts Be Gone! If you have a plantar wart, here's an easy homemade fix to do each night before bed. First, soak the affected foot in warm water for at least 10 minutes—this will soften the skin. Then, you'll need to shave off the top layer of dead skin cells to uncover the center of the wart: Rub the area with a pumice stone or emery board that you use on the wart and nothing else. Then coat the wart with hydrogen peroxide using a cotton ball or swab, and let dry for about 15 minutes. Cover up with a bandage before you go to sleep. Repeat the regimen every day, and the wart will begin to change color and eventually die off. Good riddance!

The Battle of the Boils Boils, or skin abscesses, are pimple-like skin infections that can swell into large, pus-filled, sore-to-the-touch growths. To treat a boil before it gets too big and painful to handle without a doctor, try this easy home remedy that uses tomato paste. (Yep, tomato paste!) Apply a coat of tomato paste over the boil, and the veggie's acids will lessen the pain and encourage the boil to "come to a head"—meaning, it'll soften and be ready for popping. Don't attempt to pop a boil until it's soft and you can see a small yellow dot of pus at the center.

Surprising Blister Banisher Painful blister? Try some Listerine! Antiseptic mouthwash can dry out blisters (not to mention kill germs), helping to speed the healing process. Just dab some on three times a day and cover the area with petroleum jelly. You'll be back to your summer sandals in no time.

Blister Disinfectant Blisters usually develop to protect our skin from frequent irritation—which is why we get them on our feet so often! When a blister breaks, however, the newly exposed, tender skin under the surface is susceptible to infection. To disinfect a broken blister, we like to use mouthwash, which is a strong antiseptic that can be used on the skin too. Apply mouthwash to the blister using a cotton ball, then leave uncovered to heal.

Get Rid of Splinters Lickety-Split Everybody knows the anguish caused by splinters—they're painful when stuck in your finger, and they can be excruciating to remove. Our most important tip: Don't squeeze. Instead, try this homemade splinter solution: Combine baking soda and water until you have a thick paste-like mixture. Apply to the affected area, and wait several hours until the splinter works its way out of the skin.

Relief for Bee Stings Nobody likes a bee sting, but sometimes they're inevitable. Bring down the pain and swelling by rubbing some raw onion on the sting. The sulfur in the onion will detoxify the area and give you relief.

Best a Bee Sting Ouch! Suffering from a bee or wasp sting? Soothe the pain with Vicks VapoRub. It contains menthol, which will provide a natural, cooling anesthetic effect.

who knew? THE BIG QUESTION

Relieving Bug Bites

How do you keep a mosquito bite from itching? **—Dana Ratcliffe Curtis, via Facebook**

Try a Little Toothpaste There are a ton of home remedies for mosquito bites. One of our favorites is rubbing the bite with toothpaste. Fluoride works as an antihistamine, and the mint will soothe the itchiness. Both gel and paste varieties will work equally well.

Another Fix in Your Medicine Cabinet You may have heard that hemorrhoid cream can relieve under-eye puffiness, but did you know it could also help your bug bites? Applied topically, it will reduce the pain and the swelling of an insect bite.

A Curry-ous Cure Another way to reduce the pain from mosquito bites is with a paste of curry powder and water. Apply it to the bite and let dry, then wash off. The spices in the curry powder will relieve discomfort and swelling.

Milk of Magnesia for Mosquito Bites Want to eliminate the itch from a bug bite? Look no further than the milk of magnesia in your medicine cabinet. Dab a little bit on the spot, and the antacid will stop the itchiness in its tracks.

Whip It Good Covered in mosquito bites? Stop the itch with a surprising ingredient: whipped topping. The same nondairy topping that you'd use for ice cream or pies also helps stop insect bites from being so darn itchy.

A Clearly Good Cure for Chigger Bites If you have the unfortunate experience of getting chigger bites, try painting over the bites with clear nail polish. You'll suffocate the little buggers, so that your fierce itchiness will subside.

Poison Ivy? To help relieve the itching of a rash caused by poison ivy, soak the affected area in a strong salt bath. Make sure the water is warm to fully get the itch out.

Mouth Matters

Germ Control for Your Teeth Get a head start on flu and cold season by giving your toothbrushes a thorough disinfecting on a regular basis. Soak the bristles in a small cup of hydrogen peroxide for five minutes once a week; rinse the brush thoroughly and let dry uncovered (covering the brush only retains moisture and promotes bacteria growth). If someone in your house is already sick, give all toothbrushes a peroxide bath after every time they're used.

Chamomile for Canker Sores The same chamomile tea that soothes a sour stomach can also calm canker sores. Allow the tea to cool, and then swish it around your mouth for a minute. Chamomile contains chamazulene, a natural anti-inflammatory agent, which will help accelerate the healing process.

A Cheap Cure for Cold Sores You can spend a lot of money on expensive cold sore remedies, or try this DIY version that will cost you mere pennies. Mix a small amount of baking soda with enough water to make a paste, and apply the paste to the cold sore. Allow it to dry, then rinse and pat dry. Repeat every day until the cold sore disappears, usually in about a week.

Who Knew? Classic Tip

Cold sore? Make it a thing of the past with honey! Just dab unpasteurized honey on the spot three times a day, and its antioxidants and enzymes will decrease inflammation and allow it to heal faster.

Denture Wash Anyone with dentures knows how costly store-bought cleaners can be. Luckily, making your own denture cleaner is super easy as well as cheap! Baking soda is the miracle disinfectant that will get your dentures bright white and completely deodorized. The tiny granules offer abrasive powers that'll get at all bits of food and dirt. Just sprinkle it onto your dental brush and get scrubbing!

Ease Digestive Issues

Help Heartburn Fast Don't spend money on expensive heartburn treatments until you've tried an inexpensive solution you may already have on hand: baking soda. Mixing just a half teaspoon of baking soda with water and drinking it can neutralize the acid that causes heartburn.

Who Knew? Classic Tip

Bloated? Try eating some pineapple. It's a diuretic that also contains helpful enzymes that speed digestion. To help a chronic problem, eat several slices (about 1 cup) each day. Or drink a daily glass of pineapple juice, which is delicious mixed with orange juice or in smoothies. Bloating and gassiness should subside within 72 hours.

Tame the Flame of Indigestion The spicy Italian food you ate for supper tasted amazing, but now your stomach is protesting. Luckily, you can help ease indigestion with your after-dinner drink. Just mix a dash of bitters with club soda. Your stomach will feel so much better you might go back for seconds!

Mix Up Some Pedialyte When your little ones are recovering from a tummy bug, you can help them feel better sooner with this homemade (and natural!) version of Pedialyte. Mix together 1 quart water, ½ cup orange juice, 2 tablespoons sugar, ¾ teaspoon baking soda, and ¼ teaspoon salt. Serve once their vomiting has stopped for a few hours. Make sure to contact a doctor if any problems persist.

Who Knew? Classic Tip

If you get nauseated every time you ride in a car, boat, or train, take some lemon wedges with you. Suck on them as you ride to relieve nausea. You can also try sucking on a piece of ginger or drinking ginger tea.

A Regular Old Remedy For occasional constipation, rely on an old-fashioned remedy your grandmother may have recommended to you: castor oil. Mix together a teaspoon castor oil with a little honey, and swallow it down. In a few hours, you're sure to have relief.

Weight-Loss Wonders

Put a Curb on Cravings According to experts in Chinese medicine, you can reduce food cravings by learning a simple acupressure technique at the Renzhong point—that little indentation under the nose and above your upper lip. Using your thumb and forefinger, quickly pinch this spot gently and repeatedly for about a minute. Once you finish, those Cheetos you had your eye on in the vending machine should not be so tempting.

Who Knew? Classic Tip

When a baking recipe calls for vegetable oil, try substituting half of the oil with applesauce. It's an easy way to reduce the fat content in your food.

Pepper Your Dishes Lose weight without lifting a pound! Derived from the plant Capsicum annuum, cayenne pepper has been reported to not only make you lose weight by elevating body temperature, but also to improve circulation and to lower cholesterol. As it's a mild stimulant, it can also be added to hot water with lemon juice as an alternative to coffee.

Lighten Up Your Dressing Homemade salad dressing is delicious, but its high oil content means it can also be fattening. To cut down on the tart taste of the vinegar, add a pinch of baking soda to the mix. That way, you can use less oil for your perfect salad topping.

Yes to Chocolate If you're a chocolate junkie but are trying to lose weight, you may be interested to hear that your favorite food may actually help you take off the pounds. Chocolate increases serotonin levels, so it can help lessen depression, stress, and other reasons why you may find yourself wanting to consume more food. The trick? You can only eat 1.4 ounces per day, preferably in the morning. (But hey, that's better than nothing!) Doctors recommend 70 percent dark chocolate for the biggest weight-loss effects.

Arthritis and Other Aches and Pains

Cure Everyday Aches If you regularly suffer from sore muscles, cramps, headaches, and other pains, a magnesium deficiency could be to blame. (Make sure to check with your doctor first.) Fortunately, it's easy to boost your body's stores of magnesium by a third, just by soaking in Epsom salts a few times a week. The mineral is easily absorbed by the skin, and is great for fighting aches and pains, particularly after strenuous exercise. Just add ¼ to ½ cup to your bathwater before getting in the bath.

Who Knew? Classic Tip

Believe it or not, you can help relieve arthritis pain with oatmeal. Just mix 2 cups oatmeal with 1 cup water, warm the mixture in the microwave, and apply to the affected area.

Hot Potato! Ease a sore neck with the help of a potato-turned-heating pad. First, pierce it in several places with a fork, then heat it in the microwave on high for two to three minutes, or until warm. Wrap it in a dishtowel and place on aches and pains. The warmth will ease sore muscles, and will last up to half an hour!

Grapes are Great! If you suffer from backaches or other chronic pain, try snacking on an unlikely superfood: grapes! Red grapes relax blood vessels and improve blood flow, which can help your pain. Eat 1 cup each day to see the maximum benefits.

who knew? THE BIG QUESTION

Helping Backaches

Do you have any tips to help my husband with his back pain?

—Irena Kolishchava, via Facebook

Back Pain? Check Your Wallet When men suffer from back pain, oftentimes their wallets are to blame. Sitting on a bulky wallet can cause your spine to become misaligned and your muscles to compensate. Try carrying your wallet in a front pocket (where it's also safer from pickpockets), or make sure it's as thin as possible.

Mustard Magic If you have chronic back pain—especially associated with arthritis—or other sore muscles, try adding yellow mustard to a hot bath. Add a few tablespoons for mild pain, and up to a whole 8-ounce bottle if the pain is severe. The bathwater may look strange, but your aching back will thank you.

Desk Discomfort If you think sitting at a desk might be causing lower back pain, try slightly elevating your feet. An old phone book is perfect for the job.

Forget the creams Topical sports creams are designed to ease sore, stiff backs, right? Unfortunately, they don't do much other than cause a chemical reaction that leaves your skin (but not the underlying muscles) feeling warm or cold. Don't waste your money!

Help for Leg Cramps Did you know that tomato juice can help leg cramps? The potassium in tomatoes helps ease tight muscles! Drink a glass of tomato juice each day and after a week or so you should feel a decrease in leg pain.

Castor Oil for Cramps You may be familiar with castor oil as a home remedy for constipation, but did you know that it can also help with menstrual cramps? When applied to the skin, the acids in the oil can reduce pain. Soak a rag or paper towel in castor oil and apply it to the abdomen, cover the towel with plastic wrap, then apply a heating pad. The pain should subside within 30 minutes.

First Aid Fixes

Sanitize a Cut You just got a nasty cut on your hand, but don't have anything to clean it out with before you put the bandage on. Luckily, there's something in your medicine cabinet that you may not have thought of—mouthwash. The alcohol-based formula for mouthwash was originally used as an antiseptic during surgeries, so it will definitely work for your cut, too.

For a Cozy Cool Here's a great DIY ice pack: Take a regular sponge (not the scrubbing variety), and soak it in a mixture of half water, half rubbing alcohol (or even vodka). Place it in a Ziploc bag and freeze. Since alcohol doesn't freeze completely, the sponge will stay flexible, and will easily and comfortably wrap around your achy spots much better than a hard ice pack would. If you want, you can even freeze multiple sponges, so that when one gets warm, you can just get a replacement from the freezer.

Tiny Ice Packs Put all of those packets of ketchup, mustard, and mayonnaise you've been saving to good use by using them as mini ice packs. First, let them freeze by storing them in the freezer. Then when you or your child has a small bruise, scrape, or other boo-boo tape them onto the spot with some medical or masking tape.

Rx Vinegar White vinegar stops nosebleeds. Just dampen a cotton ball and plug the nostril. The acetic acid in the vinegar cauterizes the wound. Who knew?

Comfortably Numb A spoonful of sugar may make the medicine go down, but so does an ice cube. If you suck on an ice cube for 30 seconds before taking an unpleasant liquid medicine, your mouth will be numb, and you won't be as bothered by the flavor. Great for when you need some cough syrup but are dreading the taste!

Who Knew? Classic Tip

You put a Band-Aid on your finger to cover up a scratch, but you still have to go through your day full of hand-washing, child-bathing, and dishes-doing. To keep the bandage dry while you work, cover it with a noninflated balloon—any color will do!

Splinter Removal Made Easy The easiest way to remove a splinter? Just put a drop of white glue over the offending piece of wood in your finger, let it dry, and then peel off the dried glue. The splinter will stick to the glue and come right out.

Thank You, Honey Did you know that honey has been used as an antibacterial since Roman times? Recent studies have shown that it really does help disinfect and heal burns. On a piece of sterile gauze, place a dollop of honey and apply directly on the burn. Change the dressing three to four times a day.

chapter 13

Smart Pet Tricks

Natural Remedies for Pet Health

Making Pet Cleanup Easy

Food and Drink Fixes

Fixing Pet Behavior Problems

Common Pet Problems, Solved

Natural Remedies for Pet Health

Help for Itchy Dogs If your dog has itchy skin, try this soothing oatmeal scrub. In the food processor, grind 1 to 2 cups oatmeal (the amount depends on the size of your dog). Add enough cool water to make a paste, and rub the mixture into his skin. After five to 10 minutes, wash it off with warm water, and your pooch should be scratching less often. If not, it's time to check in with the vet.

One Cool Cat Just like humans, cats can suffer in hot temperatures. But unfortunately, cats can't sweat to keep them cool. Help keep your feline friend comfortable during heat waves by wetting her paws and the tips of her ears.

Itchy Paw Pleaser After playing in the park, your dog keeps licking his paws. It might be an allergic reaction to something he stepped on outside. In a spray bottle, mix together ¼ cup cider vinegar with ½ cup water, and spray the mixture on the bottom of his paws. Vinegar will help neutralize any irritants and soothe the skin. If this tip doesn't work, or if the skin is broken, contact the vet.

For Furry Flakes To eliminate dog dandruff, massage a few tablespoons warm coconut oil into your pet's fur. Wait 15 minutes, and then shampoo it out. Coconut oil will moisturize and exfoliate your pet's skin, and can be found at most health-food stores.

Soothe a Scrape If your pet has a minor cut or scrape, apply a little aloe vera gel to the area. Not only will it have a soothing effect, but it will also fight infection and help the wound heal faster. Remember that it's always a good idea to check with your vet first.

Pad-icure Many dogs love to play outside in the snow, but their paws can cause them pain if ice starts to build up between their pads. Before heading out for a winter walk, rub some petroleum jelly between each pad. The ice will stay away and your dog can enjoy the outdoors!

Doggie Diet How-to Your vet has suggested switching your dog from wet to dry food, but your pooch seems to prefer the wet variety. Make the switch gradually by mixing the two, and slowly wean him off of the wet stuff. You might try stirring in a little plain yogurt to offset any stomach problems associated with changing brands.

who knew? THE BIG QUESTION

Eliminating Fleas

How do I know if my dog has fleas?

—Rishi Patel, via Facebook

How do you get rid of fleas?

—Jennifer Powell, via Facebook

A Test for Fleas If your dog's been scratching himself, but you're not entirely sure if she's got fleas, give her the white sock test. Slip a white sock over your hand and run it over her coat, as well as her bedding and on any carpet that she frequently lays on. If you find any little black specks on the sock, they're likely flea droppings, and you should talk to your vet.

Get Rid of Fleas You can remove pesky fleas from your pet's coat without having to pay for expensive flea collars or medications. Simply bathe your pet in salt water, and the fleas will stay away. You can also try steeping rosemary in warm water and using that as bathwater. Better yet, use a combination of the two.

Fragrant Flea Prevention Prevent fleas with eucalyptus oil! In a spray bottle, combine a few drops of the eucalyptus essential oil with 1 cup water. Use it to spray your pet's bed and other areas of your home. The fleas find eucalyptus repellent, so they'll steer clear. Don't use this spray undiluted or directly on your pet, and make sure to check with your vet first.

Hot Dog Help If your dog appears overheated, get him cooled down quickly by wiping his paws with a pad soaked in rubbing alcohol. As the alcohol evaporates, he'll start to cool down. If his condition doesn't improve quickly, call the vet, since he may be at risk for heatstroke.

Who Knew? Classic Tip

If you have both cats and dogs, you may be tempted to feed your cat dog food. Don't do it! Besides being highly insulted if he happens to see the can, your cat needs certain nutrients that are found only in food made specifically for cats.

Restore Regularity with Banana It's unpleasant, but it happens: Your dog has diarrhea. Get your dog's digestive tract back in order with some banana. Mash up two small slices for small dogs, three for medium dogs, and four for large dogs. Check with your vet first to make sure he or she is on board.

Pepto for Your Pooch It may surprise you, but most vets prescribe Pepto Bismol for doggy diarrhea. Check with your vet for the appropriate dose for your pet's weight. (Never give Pepto to cats; it's toxic for them.)

Keep It Moving Relieve doggie constipation with canned pumpkin! Plain canned pumpkin (not the seasoned pie-filling variety) can help your dog be more regular. Just double-check with your vet first to make sure he or she approves.

Who Knew? Classic Tip

If you have a cat who frequently vomits, you should (of course) take her to the vet. Unfortunately, your vet might tell you that some cats just throw up a lot. (Why do we love them so much again?) If your cat frequently vomits, try pulverizing some mint with some fresh catnip and seeing if she'll eat it—mint is good for calming stomachs.

Help Prevent Ear Infections If your poor pup is prone to uncomfortable ear infections, try this tip for keeping his ears clean. Twice a month, wipe down the inside of the ears with a cotton ball soaked in witch hazel. The astringent will help loosen wax and reduce the incidence of infection. Just be sure to ask your vet first!

Eliminate Ear Mites Naturally For a natural ear mite treatment for your pet, mix together 1 tablespoon olive oil and two to three drops liquid garlic (found at health-food stores). With an ear dropper, apply several drops to each ear daily for a month. The combination of the oil and garlic will smother and kill the mites. You may want to double check with your vet to make sure he or she approves.

Hide the Evidence To make sure your dog actually swallows his medication instead of leaving it behind in his food dish, make him a (tiny) peanut butter sandwich! Cut out two small pieces of bread, around an inch square, and spread with peanut butter. Hide the pill inside, and give it to your dog, who will gobble it up without even noticing he just ate a pill.

Who Knew? Classic Tip

If you have trouble getting your cat to swallow pills, try rubbing them in butter first. It will make them taste better to your cat, and they'll slide right down his throat.

A Cure for the Common Cold Pets get colds too! To help them get better fast, brew some elderberry tea, and put the liquid in their water bowl, ½ cup at a time. Many holistic vets believe in this remedy, but you should double check with your own pet's doc before brewing up a cup.

Pet Acne Solution If your pet sometimes suffers from chin acne, it may be caused by food particles left on his chin after he eats. Wipe his chin twice a day with a paper towel or cotton ball moistened with hydrogen peroxide and the little bumps should go away. Changing his bowl from plastic or metal to ceramic can also help the problem.

Cotton-Loving Cat? Does your cat enjoy chewing on cotton shirts and blankets? He may have a fiber deficiency. Give him the kind of fiber he needs (the dietary kind) by finely chopping some romaine lettuce and putting it in his wet food. Make sure to ask a vet before you change your pet's diet.

Making Pet Cleanup Easy

Car Seat Pet Protectors Before letting your furry friends into the car, place a bath mat on the seats for protection from dirty paws. The mat's nonslip rubber underside will help it stay put.

Deodorize Pet Stains If your pet accidentally peed on your rug, and it still smells like urine after you've cleaned it, try deodorizing the spot with club soda, which contains odor-fighting minerals. Pour some on the area, leave it for five minutes, then blot and allow to dry.

Baby Your Dog's Bed To give your dog's bed a quick clean, wipe it down with baby wipes. The alcohol will kill germs and the scent will freshen it up. Quick and easy!

Who Knew? Classic Tip

If the smell from your in-heat housecat's spray has more than nine lives, try mixing 1 cup hydrogen peroxide with ½ tablespoon baking soda and 2 squirts liquid dish soap. Pour into a spray bottle and use wherever Fluffy has left her trademark. (Be sure to spot-check as you run the risk of bleaching certain materials.)

The Ultimate Skunk Spray Remover This no-fail way to get a skunk smell out of a pet's fur was developed by a chemist as an industrial cleaner for a sulfur compound, then adapted by his coworker to solve a skunk problem! Published in the Chicago Tribune in the '90s, here it is: Mix together 2 (500 milliliter) bottles of hydrogen peroxide 3 percent solution, ¼ cup baking soda, and 2 tablespoons liquid hand soap. Add some warm water if you have a large dog. Pour over your pet, being careful to keep the solution away from his eyes. (It won't harm your pet's eyes, but it will sting!) Let sit for five minutes, or until the smell is gone. You may need to repeat in some areas if they got heavily skunked!

Who Knew? Classic Tip

Uh-oh, guests are on their way and you've just realized that your beloved cat has made a cat-fur nest all over your couch. For a quick and easy way to remove pet hair from furniture, turn to your rubber dishwashing gloves. Just slip them on, then rub the offending furniture with them. The hair will stick to the gloves and you can quickly throw it away.

Pick of the Litter (Box) You may have seen those expensive "mess free" litter boxes that cut down on the amount of litter your cat tracks around your home by making the entrance/exit to the litter box a hole on top of the cover. But did you realize you can make the same thing at home for about a quarter of what you'd pay at a pet store or other big-box retailer? All you need is an 18-gallon plastic storage container with lid. On the box's lid, trace the outline of a plate, and with a sturdy pair of scissors, cut out the circle you traced. This will be the opening for the cat to enter and exit the box. Now fill the empty storage container with cat litter and put the lid on top. You're all set with a very private, mess-free, odor-reducing litter box!

Proper Care for Pet Toys Keep your pets' playthings clean and free from bacteria and germs by tossing them into the dishwasher alone (without dishes) once a month. But hold the detergent: Just turn the temp to hot and the heat plus the water pressure will completely sanitize plastic or rubber toys. And not only will a quick wash help ensure that Fido stays healthy, it'll also prolong the life of the toys and keep your floors, carpets, and furniture clean too.

No More Fuzzy View If you have a cat who loves looking out the window, you know how full of cat hair the screen can get when he presses himself against it for a closer look outside. An easy fix? Just run a lint roller across the screen, or press a piece of tape against it.

Food and Drink Fixes

Easy-Cleaning Food Dish Keep your furry friend's food dish free from yucky stuck-on bits of wet food. Just apply cooking spray to the dish before adding the food, and any leftover clumps will stay loose and easy to clean rather than sticking to the bowl. As a bonus, the oil in the cooking spray will help nourish your pet's coat and protect his skin!

Bowl to Go Taking your pet on a camping trip, hike, or other expedition? Create an on-the-go water bowl with two empty gallon jugs of water. First, cut off the bottom part of one jug, about a third of the way up. This will be the "bowl." Then fill the second jug with water. The water jug will fit perfectly inside the bowl for storage! If you wish, you can even use a third jug bottom to make a food bowl as well.

Who Knew? Classic Tip

If your pet's food dish always ends up three feet from where it started by the time he's done eating, make it skid-proof. With a glue gun, make a thin strip of glue around the bottom rim. When dry, the hardened glue will prevent the bowl from slipping so much across the floor.

For a Happy Cat at Dinnertime Cats are very sensitive about their whiskers—if you had whiskers, you would be too! But some cats are so sensitive that they don't like eating out of food bowls that rub against their delicate whiskers. If your cat seems to have trouble at feeding time, only eating a few bits of food and then stepping back, change up her dish to change her behavior. Use a coffee can lid or shallow plate and she'll be more comfortable.

Who Knew? Classic Tip

In the hot summer months, you'd like to be able to give your dog a drink of water when you're out for a walk, but you haven't yet perfected how to train him to drink from a water fountain. Solve the problem by bringing a plastic shower cap with you. When you fill it with water it will expand enough that you can hold it out as a bowl.

Fix a Water Dish Problem Lucky you! Your pet's new trick is flipping over the water dish. Get one step ahead of him by putting his water in a heavy glass pie plate or baking dish, which he won't ever be able to lift. Problem solved!

Stay, Bowl! To keep your dog from bunting his water bowl around the yard, use a Bundt pan instead of a regular dog food dish. Drive a stake through the middle and into the ground, and there'll be no more sliding around like a hockey puck or flipping it over.

Fixing Pet Behavior Problems

Chewing Puppy Prevention If you have a new puppy, you know how much they like to chew your shoes, kids' toys—anything they can get their mouths around! Keep them from chewing up everything you own with a simple vinegar spray. Just mix equal parts white vinegar, apple cider vinegar, and water in a spray bottle and spray it on anything that needs saving. Your dog won't like the odor and will choose his chew toys instead.

Get a Cat in Its Carrier It's your least favorite part of going to the vet: getting your scaredy cat into his carrier. Instead of trying to coax your cat in, turn the carrier on its end so that the opening faces up. Then pick up the cat by the scruff and lower him in feet first. Close the door, turn the crate upright, and head to the car. You'll help outsmart your cat's fear, and end up with fewer scratches in the process!

For Better Bathroom Habits Your cat seems to have taken a vacation from the litter box, and you're finding unpleasant surprises in interesting places like the bathtub. To fix this problem, try placing a bowl of food in the places where you've found those surprises. Cats don't do their business in the same place that they eat, so she'll hopefully find her way back to the litter box. If not, call your vet to make sure she's not suffering from any health problems.

Who Knew? Classic Tip

If your dog simply won't come when called, it might be time to start from scratch. Once a dog has decided that a word doesn't mean anything to him, it's much harder to make him understand that "come" means "come to me," not "do whatever you want." Pick a different word like "here" or "move," and begin your dog's training over again by standing several feet away, saying your new word, and offering treats when he obeys. Your friends at the dog park might think it's weird when you shout, "Draw nigh, Rover!" but it's way better than having him run the other way.

Happy Tails Distraction is sometimes the best medicine when it comes to behavior modification for pets. Head off trouble by shaking coins in a metal can when you see your furry friend about to jump headlong into a spot where he shouldn't be or a dinner plate that isn't for him.

Get Your Dog to Come Back If you have trouble getting your dog to come back after you've taken him off his leash in a forest or off-the-leash dog park, here's a bit of dog psychology that will help: Many dogs are more likely to come if they think you're playing, rather than commanding. Instead of yelling at your pooch to come back, call his name playfully and run the other way. Chances are, he'll run after you, and you can clip his leash back on when he catches up.

Deter Cat Scratch Fever Cats are wonderful pets, but all their scratching can do serious damage to your home! To keep your kitties from digging their claws into furniture, walls, or anything else, swipe a bit of VapoRub on their favorite scratching targets. Cats hate the cough medicine's mentholated smell and they won't get within a sniff's distance.

Protect Your Pet from Cords Stop your pet's dangerous habit of chewing on electric cords by rubbing them with a little soap. The soap won't harm your cat or dog, but it will certainly send them in search of a tastier chew toy.

A Red-Hot Repellent For some reason, your dog finds your shoes more appealing than any of his chew toys. Break the attraction by mixing together a little cayenne pepper and Vaseline, and swipe a little on whichever part of the shoe that he bites. The hot pepper will deter him, but it won't cause any health problems. Just be sure to check with your vet to make sure this tip is safe for your pet.

Who Knew? Classic Tip

If your cat seems to think your potted plant is a fun place to hang out—or worse, a good place to go to the bathroom, use some thyme to help her find some other place to play. Sprinkle dried thyme on the surface of the soil once a week. She won't like the strong scent and won't want to put her paws in it.

Keep a Cat Off Furniture If there's a specific piece of furniture you don't want your cat on or a place you don't want him to go, you know how hard it is to enforce this rule. If your yelling doesn't seem to be much of a deterrent to your favorite feline, try this instead: In a spray bottle, mix together ½ cup water with ⅛ teaspoon cinnamon, and shake to combine. Cats hate the smell of cinnamon, so if you spray this where you don't want him to go, he should stay away.

who knew? THE BIG QUESTION

Keeping Pets Calm

My dog is such a scaredy cat! Is there any way to keep him from being so jittery?

—Christine Dugan-Hart, via Facebook

Keep the Calm with Chamomile To keep your dog calm while you're traveling, spray his carrier or seat with some chamomile tea. The scent has a relaxing effect (even for pets!), and you'll be able to spend more time focusing on the road, not on what your dog is doing.

The Scent of a Dog Owner Don't toss those old sweatpants! Put them in your dog's bed, and he'll stay calmer and sleep better, having the scent of you nearby. This trick is also useful if you're going on a trip—any clothing piece will do!

It's Electric! If your dog gets antsy during storms, surprisingly, it might not be the storm itself that's bothering him, but the buildup of static electricity in his fur. Rub him down with a dryer sheet to eliminate the problem. This is also a great tip for dry winter days.

Aromatherapy for Separation Anxiety If your dog gets anxious whenever you leave your home, try calming him down with a little aromatherapy. In a spray bottle, combine several drops lavender essential oil with a cup of water, and spray his pet bed and favorite spots with it. Lavender has a calming effect on dogs and humans alike. Avoid this tip if you have cats, as lavender essential oil can be harmful to them.

Common Pet Problems, Solved

Make a Cozier Cat Bed Cats are drawn to warm spots, so if you'd rather yours spend the night in her own bed and not climb on top of you while you sleep, try this tip. Set a heating pad under a towel on the floor or wherever you'd like your pet to sleep. Turn it on low heat and leave it on for 10 to 15 minutes, or until it seems like your cat has settled in for the night. You'll create a warm space she loves to cuddle up on.

Keep Small Animals Calm If you have a rabbit, guinea pig, hamster, or other small pet who lives in a cage, try refilling his water dish by sticking a turkey baster through the bars. It will allow you to give him something fresh to drink without scaring him by opening the door and moving things around.

A Bath for Your Goldfish Before you clean out your goldfish's bowl, first prepare a saltwater bath for him. Even though goldfish are freshwater fish, salt will help your fish absorb much-needed electrolytes and kill any parasites on his fins. To get the saltwater ready, run tap water into a bowl and let it sit for a day to allow the chlorine to evaporate (you should do this when filling his freshwater bowl too). Add a teaspoon of non-iodized salt and mix until it dissolves. Then let Goldy go for a swim in the saltwater for approximately 15 minutes.

Long-Lasting Dog Tags Prevent rust on your dog's tags by polishing them with car wax. Reapply every few months, and they'll last much longer!

Who Knew? Classic Tip

The best time to clip your dog's nails is after he's had a bath or has been swimming. The water will soften the hard outer coating of your pet's nails, making them easier to cut.

A Speedier Doggie Bath There's nothing quite like wrestling a sudsy, wet dog in the bathtub! To help rinse the shampoo out of his coat more quickly, rinse him with ½ cup cider vinegar mixed in 5 cups water. It will break down the suds, making your job easier. Any remaining vinegar odor will disappear when the fur dries.

Quieter Dog Days It's great that your loyal canine is always by your side, but you could do without the accompanying jingle jangle of his ID and rabies tags. The same colorful vinyl caps that you use to easily identify keys will work to silence those ringing tags. Now the dogs can be like the kids—seen and not heard. (We can dream.)

Who Knew? Classic Tip

Is your dog leaving brown spots on your lawn where he decides to pee? Put a few drops of vinegar into his water bowl every time you refill it and brown spots will be a thing of the past.

Dogs Have Bad-Hair Days Too! If your dog's coat is looking frizzy, give him a good brushing and rub him down with a little bit of aloe vera gel. The aloe will help keep the fur moisturized so that his coat looks shiny again.

Hot Dog Worried about your pooch getting overheated, or worse, bored this summer? Freeze water and chicken stock with his favorite toys and treats and solve both problems at the same time!

Index